STRONGER

A simple guide
for connecting with God

Yet those who wait for the LORD Will gain new strength;
They will mount up with wings like eagles, They will run and not get tired,
They will walk and not become weary.

Isaiah 40:31 (NASB)

Written by CJ Rapp and Pam Marotta

CJ.rapp
MINISTRIES

Published by Infusion Publishing™
A ministry of CJ Rapp Ministries. www.cjrapp.com
Mission Viejo, CA 92692
Phone: 949-954-4237

Edited by Teresa Haymaker

First edition, 2015
ISBN: 978-0-9824790-2-5
Printed in the United States of America

Scripture quotations marked AMP are from the *Amplified Bible*, Copyright © 1954, 1958, 1962, 1964, 1965, 1987 The Lockman Foundation. Used by permission.

Scripture quotations marked ESV are taken from *The Holy Bible*, English Standard Version. Copyright © 2000; 2001 by Crossway Bibles, a division of Good News Publishers. Used by permission. All rights reserved.

Scripture quotations marked GW are from GOD'S WORD. GOD'S WORD is a copyrighted work of God's Word to the Nations Bible Society. Quotations are used by permission. Copyright 1995 by God's Word to the Nations Bible Society. All rights reserved.

Scripture quotations marked KJV are taken from the *King James Version* of the Bible. The King James Version is in the public domain in the United States; you may copy and quote from it without restriction.

Scripture quotations marked NASB are taken from *New American Standard Bible*, Copyright © 1960, 1962, 1963, 1968, 1971, 1972, 1973, 1975, 1977, 1995 by The Lockman Foundation. Used by permission.

Scripture quotations marked NKJV are from the *NEW KING JAMES VERSION*. Copyright © 1979, 1980, 1982 by Thomas Nelson, Inc. Used by permission. All rights reserved.

Scripture quotations marked NIV are from the *Holy Bible, New International Version*®. Copyright © 1973, 1978, 1984, by International Bible Society. Used by permission of Zondervan Publishing House. All rights reserved.

Scripture quotations marked NLT are taken from the *Holy Bible, New Living Translation*, copyright © 1996. Used by permission of Tyndale House Publishers, Inc., Wheaton, IL 60189. All rights reserved.

Scripture quotations marked TLB are taken from *The Living Bible* copyright © 1971. Used by permission of Tyndale House Publishers, Inc., Carol Stream, Illinois 60188. All rights reserved.

Scripture quotations marked *The Message*. Copyright © by Eugene H. Peterson 193, 1994, 1995, 196, 2000, 2001, 2002. Used by permission of NavPress Publishing Group.

Contents

Dedicated to the best team
of Jesus followers ever…
Karrie, Francesca, Pam,
Julie and our Larry.
Grateful for our journey together.

A Note From CJ

Hello!

I'm excited you've decided to take the same journey my friends and I experienced almost a year ago. *STRONGER* came about as a result of our collective belief that the strength we all need for life's up and downs must flow from our relationship with God. We were worn out, exhausted, too busy, stressed and simply feeling overwhelmed with life. Spending intentional time with the Lord got pushed to the back burner as we ran to put out the fires of everyday life. Then one day as Karrie was reading Isaiah 40:31 she felt the Lord impressing her to stop running and start resting. She was to wait, not just on him, but in him...just like she would if she were sitting in an easy chair.

> *Yet those who wait for the LORD will gain new strength;*
> *They will mount up with wings like eagles,*
> *They will run and not get tired,*
> *They will walk and not become weary.*

Isaiah 40:31 (NASB)

She shared her revelation with our group and at first we thought she was crazy. How could we rest when we were busy wives, busy moms, busy business executives, and busy launching a national conference series? And, did I mention we were busy? As the weeks went by we noticed new life flowing from Karrie. She was peaceful, energetic, incredibly creative, and steadfast in faith despite growing business tensions. Finally, we asked her what she was doing, because whatever it was, we needed it. She said, "I am finding new strength as I rest and wait on the Lord." Desperate to experience the same dramatic difference as Karrie, we started to practice resting together.

To be clear, that did not mean ceasing all activity and abandoning work and responsibilities. It did mean being intentional. This resting produced the same outcome in our lives as it did in hers. We learned to make space for God and we each experienced his presence and power in a whole new way. Because we are all so different, *rest* looks different for each of us. We let go of our preconceived expectations about what quiet time should look like. We began to talk about what it really means to have a relationship with God. We dared to believe we could know Jesus as our friend, someone we could talk with, not at, and hear his response. We shared what was working, what we were learning and how we were growing in, what we began to call, our *Strength Training* exercises.

God did something amazing...*he met us* where we were. We experienced personal breakthroughs, we found the strength to forgive old hurts and let go of our hang ups. We discovered a newfound peace, not that life settled down, because it didn't; we just learned to focus on his presence in the midst of the chaos. In short, this journey so profoundly affected our lives we knew we had to share this simple guide for connecting with God. We watched in awe as God continued to move in the hearts of people who joined us on our journey.

Over the next few weeks you'll be stepping out with your group as you begin to practice *Strength Training*. You'll have your own unguarded conversations about your time with God and what it means to have a relationship with him. At times you may find it hard and maybe even a bit frustrating, but stick with it. Strength is built by adding a resistance. With every day that passes you will learn more about God's heart for you and his desire to spend time with you—his beloved.

Strength Training alongside you!

CJ

WHAT IS *STRONGER*

So now that you know what inspired *STRONGER*, what exactly can you expect from the next six weeks of *STRONGER*?

A Growing Relationship with God. When it comes to relationship with God all of us enter this amazing, ongoing, growing journey by stepping into the unknown. At the moment you started following Jesus you entered into a personal intimate relationship with the Living God, Father, Son, and Holy Spirit whether you knew it or not. This relationship was more than your mind and understanding could conceive. It's a relationship with benefits!

- You received a new heart and a mind that can be renewed!
- A direct line to the throne room of God!
- The power and strength you need for living each day fueled by the promise of his presence every second you live!
- A guide for life in the Holy Spirit who took up residence in your heart!
- Spiritual gifts that will propel your life in an unimaginable direction.

STRONGER will help you maximize these benefits by showing you simple ways to recognize and depend upon them in your everyday life.

A Simple Guide to Help you Connect with Him

When beginning a relationship with the Lord we are often given a checklist of how to have a relationship with God:

- ☐ Go to church
- ☐ Read the Bible
- ☐ Pray
- ☐ Quiet time
- ☐ Memorize Verses
- ☐ Tithe
- ☐ Serve others

Unfortunately, while these are important "to do's" they leave many people feeling guilty. Even the contemporary term "quiet time" often becomes just another box to check off in our already overscheduled day. This leads to disillusionment and frustration. We realize our relationships are not changing, we are not growing, and we are not experiencing the personal presence and power we read about in the pages of the Bible; and we wonder if God is real, and if so, why am I not experiencing Christ in me?

My friend, Tim Timmons, Jr., wrestles with these thoughts in his song *Christ in Me*:

> The same great light that broke the dark
> The same great peace that calmed the seas
> Hallelujah, is living in me
> The same great love that gives us breath
> The same great power that conquered death
> Hallelujah, is flowing through me

And what, what if I believed in Your power,
And I really lived it?
What, what if I believed Christ in me?
What if I believe?

I would lay my worries down
See these hills as level ground
What if I believed Christ in me?

The same great love that casts out fear
The same compassion that draws us near
Hallelujah, is living in me, yeah, yeah!
The same great mercy that I received
Amazing grace for a wretch like me
Hallelujah, is flowing through me

Oh, I would praise You with my life
Let my story lift You high
What if I believed Christ in me?
Oh, what if I believed Christ in me?

And what, what if I believed in Your power?
And what, what if I believed Christ in me?
What if I believe?*

---

*   Tim Timmons, Alli Rogers, *Let's Be Beautiful*, Sony/ATV Cross Keys Publishing, Sony/ATV Timber Publishing, West Main Music.

But what if we *could* be the kind of people Jesus talks about in John 14:12?

I tell you the truth, anyone who believes in me will do the same works I have done, and even greater works, because I am going to be with the Father.

John 14:12 (NLT)

What if the list we received with our new believer packets wasn't what we need to do, but what we need to be?

This is what *STRONGER* is all about!

STRONGER is *A Simple Guide for Connecting with God*. To borrow from a cultural icon you might call it "Relationship with God for Dummies." Whatever labels we put on this study, we are convinced if you give yourself fully to *Strength Training* and truly pursue God over the next six weeks and beyond you will:

- Gain strength and the power you need to face the ups and downs of each day.
- Grow in your understanding of God's love, power, and provision for your life.
- Grow in your ability to discern God's voice.
- Experience greater intimacy with the Lord.

Strength Training Coaching

We use *Strength Training* as a picture of building *a stronger relationship* with God. Just as we must keep our muscles strong by exercising and using them, we must also practice and strength train our spiritual muscles. You'll find simple ideas to help you connect with God in a way that works for YOU. There will be no pressure, no guilt, just an honest exploration of what it means to have a very real relationship with God.

ABOUT THIS GUIDEBOOK

This simple guide contains six lessons. We suggest you grab your closest friends and cheer for each other as you strength train. To the person who is a Lone Ranger, we remind you that even he had Tonto, Batman had Robin, John had Ponch (ChIPs), Han Solo had Chewbacca and Captain Jack Sparrow had Mr. Gibbs. In other words, we are not meant to do life alone, we need the support of one another to grow (Ecclesiastes 4:9–12).

WHAT'S INSIDE?

In every lesson you will find the following sections. Keep in mind that each lesson builds on the one that came before it. If you miss a week make sure you go back and complete what you missed.

FOCUS

This section turns your attention to and motivates you for what is coming. It gives you an idea of what you can expect and it helps you define why each topic is important for you. It includes exercises and questions that make you think! They will help you gauge where you are in your journey with God. It allows for personal evaluation—no right or wrong answers just an honest evaluation of where you are.

EXPLORE

Here we present what God has to say in the Bible about what we are learning. We'll explore what we think about it and how it applies to us.

GOD'S HEART FOR YOU

A Scripture based prayer written as God's thoughts and desire for you.

SHARE

To get you started with a meaningful time of discussion together, we suggest you review the questions scattered throughout each lesson. Consider the needs of your group when picking questions. Keep in mind, connecting with God is personal. This is a personal journey, not a one size fits all.

STRENGTH TRAINING

This section is a guide for your personal time with the Lord at home, or wherever you are comfortable spending the time. Participation is the key to transformation. It doesn't matter where you are; in the car, pulling weeds, or sitting in your special place. What matters is you do it. The goal of our *Strength Training* time is to:

1. Learn to consistently practice the presence of God with you.
2. Grow in the discipline of silence and solitude.
3. Tune your ear to hear his voice.
4. Deepen your friendship and grow in your relationship with God.

We'll help you with practical ideas to get you started that will demystify what it means to have a relationship with God. If you regularly meet with the Lord and can already hear him speaking to you, just proceed as you now do. If this is new to you be patient and don't get discouraged. Your biggest obstacle will be quieting your mind. Remember, our relationship with the Lord is personal. No two people will connect in exactly the same way. We encourage you to do what works best for you.

Yikes! What Do I Do if I'm a Host?

1. Don't Panic! God will show up and help you. Stress creates a tense atmosphere.

2. Invite your friends. It is *WAY* more fun to go on this journey with your friends—and it adds accountability. ☺

3. Ask everyone to pitch in—have each person volunteer to do something each week. Sharing the responsibility creates a sense of ownership for everyone and it increases participation.

4. Be familiar with the lesson and the questions that will be discussed together.

5. Don't teach. Instead, get people talking. The idea is to share and learn from each other.

6. Honor each other's time.

7. Be committed to the journey and to the small group.

Tips for Success

1. Have a real desire to grow in your relationship with the Lord.

2. The most personally powerful part of *STRONGER* is doing the exercises. The most impactful part is sharing your journey with others. Be open.

3. Ask God to reveal himself to you.

4. This book is meant to be used! Don't forget it. Mark it up—take notes—tear pages out—jot down your thoughts.

5. Don't skimp on time for the *Focus* and *Explore* sections. Don't rush through your *Strength Training*.

6. Beware of busyness! It is the enemy's attempt to keep you from growing stronger with God.

7. Engage! You'll get out of this experience what you put into it!

I JOINED THE GROUP. NOW WHAT?

1. I promise to embrace this journey with all my heart, soul, mind and strength!

2. I promise to be on time.

3. I promise I will not gossip or share anything said in our group. I will not talk about group members!

4. I will not dominate the sharing time.

5. I will not try to fix people, tell them what they should do, or teach a sermon.

6. I will only share about me—not Sally's cat, Frank's son, or my mate's flaws.

7. I will expect God to meet us right where we are!

_____   _____
My signature   Date

...those who wait for the Lord
will gain
NEW strength...

Isaiah 40:31a (NASB)

Caution: Life Altering Material Inside

LEVEL 1: STRENGTH TRAINING 101

FOCUS

If your life were a car what type of car would it be and why?

Take a look at the cover picture. Describe how it relates to your relationship with God.

What, if any, is the relationship between the type of car used to describe your life and the description of your relationship with God?

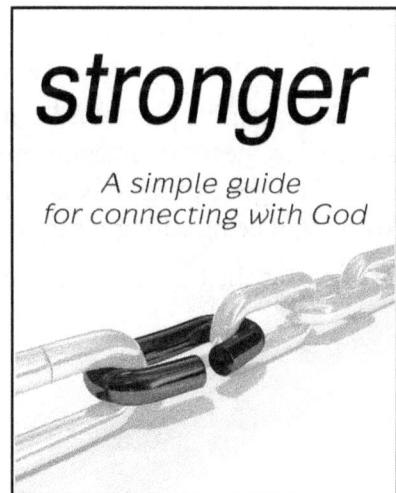

stronger

*A simple guide
for connecting with God*

Have you ever been told you are strong? Do you think of other people as strong? Ever wonder where their strength comes from?

Strength is a quality that many people value. In fact, in our culture people long to be strong. Strength training has become a multibillion dollar industry. There are pills and nutritional shakes that promise to make you stronger. There are countless work-out videos and programs aimed at building your strength. Schools offer education and certificates for people who desire to become strength trainers to assist you along your journey.

But, strength is more than a physical quality. In addition to physical strength, we need to be emotionally and mentally strong. From the time we are young we are taught to be "strong and independent." However, Paul told Timothy:

> *Train yourself toward godliness (piety), [keeping yourself spiritually fit]. For*
> *physical training is of some value (useful for a little), but godliness (spiritual*
> *training) is useful and of value in everything and in every way, for it holds promise*
> *for the present life and also for the life which is to come.*
>
> 1 Timothy 4:7b–8 (AMP)

How can spiritual training or becoming spiritually stronger benefit me? How is it useful and of value in everything and in every way? How do I train to become spiritually stronger?

When thinking about training what thoughts and pictures come to your mind? Do you think about timers, weights, water bottles, and sweaty towels? Do your muscles ache at the thought of what a training program might look like? Are you overwhelmed with thoughts of countless hours you might need to invest and how you will make the time? Do thoughts of past failed attempts at training plague you?

What if spiritual strength training was the complete opposite of physical strength training? If I told you the primary components of spiritual strength training are "waiting, resting and following" would you want to know more?

Good training programs begin with an honest assessment of your current condition. For some of us, hearing someone describe us as strong causes us to question what that means. It can be a good thing to be strong but at other times being strong might be a negative trait. What does being strong mean to you?

Look at the box on the next page. Circle the areas where you need strength.

Health Challenges   Traffic

Ministry

Your Job   *Parenting*

Finances   Marriage

Overcoming Depression

Family   *Aging Parents*

Friendships

Other_____

In your opinion, is strength a character quality, a spiritual condition, a physical description or all three? Write your thoughts below:

Physical strength is:

Emotional strength is:

Spiritual strength is:

PERSONAL STRENGTH EVALUATION

Based on your definitions, rate how strong you feel:

Physically:

WEAK   STRONG

1 2 3 4 5 6 7 8 9 10

Emotionally:

1 2 3 4 5 6 7 8 9 10

Spiritually:

1 2 3 4 5 6 7 8 9 10

While charts and self-assessments are helpful, the only way to truly evaluate one's strength is to test it.

Think back over the last twelve months. Describe a situation in which you felt strong. What caused you to feel strong? How did your strength help you in the circumstance?

For the purposes of this study, and so we can all be on the same page, let's define what it means to be strong physically, emotionally and spiritually.

- Physical strength is the quality of being physically strong bodily or muscularly; vigor (physical strength and good health).

- Emotional strength is emotional stability and resiliency; not being controlled or ruled by your emotions. Emotional strength involves mental toughness and focus as our thoughts stir up our emotions.

- Spiritual strength is the strength God provides to his people to equip them for daily life in his kingdom. It is supplied or imparted to man through the power of the Holy Spirit at work in us.

Where does strength ultimately come from? Is it something we are born with? Is it developed over time? Or does it flow from our relationship with the Lord? What do you think?

The amount of strength we have is dependent upon
our awareness of God's presence with us.

Would it surprise you to learn that the **source** of all strength—physical, emotional (heart), and spiritual—*is the Lord?*

This is why cultivating an intimate relationship with the Lord is so important!

David was King of Israel and perhaps the mightiest warrior recorded in Scripture. He was a man who worshipped God with all his heart. One of David's songs to the Lord declares *The God of Israel Himself gives strength and power to the people. Blessed be God!* Psalm 68:35b (NASB).

EXPLORE

THE BIBLE TEACHES US THAT ALL STRENGTH IS SUPPLIED BY GOD. There are many accounts in the Bible where the Lord is called our strength. Consider the following passages. Underline, highlight or note anything that stands out to you and make note of why this caught your attention. Consider sharing your thoughts with your group or a friend.

GOD IS THE SUPPLIER OF OUR PHYSICAL STRENGTH

He gives power to the faint and weary, and to him who has no might He increases strength [causing it to multiply and making it to abound]. Even youths shall faint and be weary, and [selected] young men shall feebly stumble and fall exhausted; But those who wait for the Lord [who expect, look for, and hope in Him] shall change and renew their strength and power; they shall lift their wings and mount up [close to God] as eagles [mount up to the sun]; they shall run and not be weary, they shall walk and not faint or become tired.

Isaiah 40:29–31 (AMP)

In Judges we read about a man named Samson who served as a Judge of Israel for twenty years. Samson had been set apart from birth as a Nazirite (Judges 13:1-5). As long as no razor ever cut his hair he had exceptional strength given to him by God to defeat Israel's enemies. But good old Samson had some serious moral defects, including a lust for women. In particular, Delilah was able to trick Samson into telling her the source of his strength. Of course, she revealed the secret of Samson's strength to his enemies.

As a result, they came while he slept and cut his hair. Samson was overpowered, defeated, taken captive and blinded (Judges 16:1–22). However, his story doesn't end in defeat.

> *Now the lords of the Philistines gathered to offer a great sacrifice to Dagon their god and to rejoice, and they said, "Our god has given Samson our enemy into our hand." And when the people saw him, they praised their god. For they said, "Our god has given our enemy into our hand, the ravager of our country, who has killed many of us." And when their hearts were merry, they said, "Call Samson, that he may entertain us." So they called Samson out of the prison, and he entertained them. They made him stand between the pillars. And Samson said to the young man who held him by the hand, "Let me feel the pillars on which the house rests, that I may lean against them." Now the house was full of men and women. All the lords of the Philistines were there, and on the roof there were about 3,000 men and women, who looked on while Samson entertained. Then Samson called to the LORD and said, "O Lord GOD, please remember me and please strengthen me only this once, O God, that I may be avenged on the Philistines for my two eyes." And Samson grasped the two middle pillars on which the house rested, and he leaned his weight against them, his right hand on the one and his left hand on the other. And Samson said, "Let me die with the Philistines." Then he bowed with all his strength, and the house fell upon the lords and upon all the people who were in it. So the dead whom he killed at his death were more than those whom he had killed during his life.*

Judges 16:23–30 (ESV)

Samson humbled himself and trusted in God to renew his physical strength.

We have all experienced feeling physically weak. Things like illness or injury can rob us of our strength. Do you intentionally trust in God to restore your physical strength? Can you think of a time when the Lord strengthened you physically? Describe it in a few short sentences.

GOD IS OUR EMOTIONAL STRENGTH

God is the supplier of our emotional and mental strength. In Scripture our heart is the center of our emotions and thoughts. Psalm 73:26 says, *My flesh and my heart may fail, but God is the strength of my heart and my portion forever* (NIV).

Emotions like fear, depression, anxiety, worry, anger, etc. have the ability to drain us of strength—especially when we allow them to affect our attitude and actions. In waiting on and trusting in the Lord we find strength to experience our emotions instead of being overcome by them. King David was a man who learned to process his emotions with the Lord. The Psalms are full of David's thoughts and feelings about the events of his life.

Underline, highlight or note anything that stands out to you and make note of why this caught your attention. Consider sharing your thoughts with your group or a friend.

[A Psalm] of David. THE LORD is my Light and my Salvation—whom shall I fear or dread? The Lord is the Refuge and Stronghold of my life—of whom shall I be afraid? When the wicked, even my enemies and my foes, came upon me to eat up my flesh, they stumbled and fell. Though a host encamp against me, my heart shall not fear; though war arise against me, [even then] in this will I be confident.
One thing have I asked of the Lord, that will I seek, inquire for, and [insistently] require: that I may dwell in the house of the Lord [in His presence] all the days of my life, to behold and gaze upon the beauty [the sweet attractiveness and the delightful loveliness] of the Lord and to meditate, consider, and inquire in His temple. For in the day of trouble He will hide me in His shelter; in the secret place of His tent will He hide me; He will set me high upon a rock. And now shall my head be lifted up above my enemies round about me; in His tent I will offer sacrifices and shouting of joy; I will sing, yes, I will sing praises to the Lord. Hear, O Lord, when I cry aloud; have mercy and be gracious to me and answer me! You have said, Seek My face [inquire for and require My presence as your vital need]. My heart says to You, Your face (Your presence), Lord, will I seek, inquire for, and require [of necessity and on the authority of Your Word]. Hide not Your face from me; turn not Your servant away in anger, You Who have been my help!
Cast me not off, neither forsake me, O God of my salvation! Although my father and my mother have forsaken me, yet the Lord will take me up [adopt me as His child]. Teach me Your way, O Lord, and lead me in a plain and even path because of my enemies [those who lie in wait for me]. Give me not up to the will of my adversaries,

for false witnesses have risen up against me; they breathe out cruelty and violence.
[What, what would have become of me] had I not believed that I would see the
Lord's goodness in the land of the living! Wait and hope for and expect the Lord; be
brave and of good courage and let your heart be stout and enduring.
Yes, wait for and hope for and expect the Lord.

Psalm 27:1–14 (AMP)

Nothing drains our strength quite like fear. David's enemies sought his life. He had every reason to run and hide, but instead he turned to and trusted in the Lord. Anxiety and fear did not rule him. Instead, confidence in God and his protection calmed him. God's presence resulted in David's peace. David was encouraged and his heart strengthened in God's presence.

Describe a similar time in your own life when you talked to the Lord about what you were feeling (anger, fear, sadness, etc.) and as a result felt better?

In waiting on and trusting in the Lord, we find strength
to experience our emotions instead of being overcome by them.

GOD IS OUR SPIRITUAL STRENGTH

As followers of Jesus, the Holy Spirit lives in us. It is his job to strengthen, gift, comfort, help, guide, and empower believers. Paul prayed in Ephesians 3:14–21:

For this reason [seeing the greatness of this plan by which you are built together in
Christ], I bow my knees before the Father of our Lord Jesus Christ, For Whom every
family in heaven and on earth is named [that Father from Whom all fatherhood
takes its title and derives its name]. May He grant you out of the rich treasury of
His glory to be strengthened and reinforced with mighty power in the
inner man by the [Holy] Spirit [Himself indwelling your innermost being and
personality]. May Christ through your faith [actually] dwell (settle down, abide,
make His permanent home) in your hearts! May you be rooted deep in love and
founded securely on love, That you may have the power and be strong to
apprehend and grasp with all the saints [God's devoted people, the experience of
that love] what is the breadth and length and height and depth [of it];
[That you may really come] to know [practically, through experience for yourselves]

*the love of Christ, which far surpasses mere knowledge [without experience]; that
you may be filled [through all your being] unto all the fullness of God [may have the
richest measure of the divine Presence, and become a body wholly filled
and flooded with God Himself]! Now to Him Who, by (in consequence of) the
[action of His] power that is at work within us, is able to [carry out His purpose
and] do superabundantly, far over and above all that we [dare] ask or
think [infinitely beyond our highest prayers, desires, thoughts, hopes,
or dreams]—To Him be glory in the church and in Christ Jesus
throughout all generations forever and ever. Amen (so be it).*

Ephesians 3:14–21 (AMP)

- In the verses above underline, highlight or note anything that stands out to you and make note of why this caught your attention. Consider sharing your thoughts with your group or a friend.

- Describe a time in your life when the Lord strengthened you spiritually. For example, did you feel his comfort during a difficult situation? Did he empower you to do something for him? Did he enable you to love or see someone through his eyes?

The men in each example above share one common experience—dependence upon God for strength.

- Samson prayed and asked God to make him strong one more time.

- Psalm 10:17 says, *O Lord, You have heard the desire of the humble; you will strengthen their heart* (NASB). David gives us an example of this in Psalm 28:7–8 when he said, *The LORD is my strength and shield. I trust him with all my heart. He helps me, and my heart is filled with joy. I burst out in songs of thanksgiving. The LORD gives his people strength* (NLT).

- Paul prayed that the Lord would strengthen you *with power through His Spirit in the inner man* (Ephesians 3:16 NASB).

God alone was the source of their strength—all of it. They recognized him as their supplier and called upon him for strength. But how did they know God was their supply?

> The one common thread in all the examples above, is *their personal relationship with God.* Each person had personally come to depend upon the Lord as the supplier of their strength. They were intimately aware that God's power was available when they called out to him.

If you are tempted to think God supplied his power to them because they were examples of holiness, think again. Samson was a womanizer and overconfident in his abilities. David was an adulterer and a murderer. Paul, once called Saul, was a persecutor of followers of Jesus. Human and flawed they all learned to trust and depend upon God, who in his grace and for his purposes, supplied each man with the kind of strength they needed.

What about you? Do you recognize God as the source of ALL your strength? Explain your answer.

Strength comes from our relationship with the Lord. People, in general, do not depend on someone they don't know. Through relationship we come to trust someone enough to depend upon them. Trust is the key to dependence.

But what does that look like?

> *Yet those who wait for the Lord Will gain new strength;*
> *They will mount up with wings like eagles, They will run and not get*
> *tired, They will walk and not become weary.*
>
> Isaiah 40:31 (NASB)

> The Hebrew word "wait" means: to look for eagerly,
> to hope and expect, to stay in a place of expectation.

Waiting is not traditional quiet time as we might think of it. Instead, waiting is faith in action. It is eager expectancy that God will provide the answer, strength, provision, etc.

you need. This type of trust in God is not dependent upon the outcome. It is assurance that God's *got it* no matter how it turns out.

The following verses are written by people who learned to wait on God. Make notes, underline or highlight anything you see that stands out to you.

My soul, wait silently for God alone, For my expectation is from Him.
He only is my rock and my salvation; He is my defense; I shall not be moved.
In God is my salvation and my glory; The rock of my strength, And my refuge,
is in God. Trust in Him at all times, you people; Pour out your heart
before Him; God is a refuge for us. Selah.

Psalm 62:5–8 (NKJV)

I waited patiently for the Lord; And He inclined to me, And heard my cry. He also
brought me up out of a horrible pit, Out of the miry clay, And set my feet
upon a rock, And established my steps. He has put a new song in my
mouth—Praise to our God; Many will see it and fear, And will trust in the Lord.
Blessed is that man who makes the Lord his trust, And does not respect the proud,
nor such as turn aside to lies. Many, O Lord my God, are Your wonderful works
Which You have done; And Your thoughts toward us Cannot be recounted to You in
order; If I would declare and speak of them, They are more than can be numbered.

Psalm 40:1–5 (NKJV)

Strength training is really "wait" training. Waiting is about developing intimacy with God. It is depending on him and his sufficiency and supply. It is waiting with the expectation and confidence that he hears you and will act. It is about trust. Ultimately it is about putting our trust in the love the Father has for us and his plan for our lives.

Does "waiting" mean that our body is still? Is it reasonable to think that in daily life we can do nothing but sit still before the Lord waiting and listening? In truth our bodies can be active but our soul can remain in a state of peace and trust in the Lord continually. This becomes a habitual source of spiritual strength. Are there times when we need to be still? Yes! But the point is our ongoing dependence and trust in God is the result of our soul—the inner being consisting of our mind, will and emotions—being focused on God.

Do you need new strength? Then wait—wait in the presence of the Lord. Do what David did in Psalm 27 and seek his face. *Inquire and require My presence as your vital need* (verse

8, AMP). Gaze upon the beauty of the Lord—who he is and what he has done for you. Share with him your feelings and thoughts and listen to what he says in response.

If your heart is broken and you need understanding—wait in his presence.

If you feel weak and powerless—wait in his presence.

If you are tired or exhausted—wait in his presence.

Think about the word *wait*. What if quiet time isn't a "to do" but a "to be"?

The good news is that waiting on the Lord doesn't mean life has to stop. Waiting, is an ongoing connection with God.

GOD'S HEART FOR YOU

My beautiful child, it is my joy to enable you to work alongside me as you wait expectantly for me. In your waiting patiently in my presence, I will renew your strength and fill you with joy. As you learn to draw upon my peace while you wait in my presence you will be strengthened for every task I put before you. It is walking with me, waiting on me, and by resting in me that you will discover that I freely strengthen you to do my will. I will not call you to anything that I will not equip you to do. It is my power within you that accomplishes every good work. Make no mistake; apart from me you can do nothing. I am the source of your strength. As a branch is connected to a vine and bears fruit, so you draw nourishment and strength from me. You are my instrument for my glory and I will enable you to accomplish my will for you and for those I place along your path. Together we will touch the lives of many. Rest in my presence and love! I will strengthen you to do mighty works alongside me.

~~~~~~~~~~

Refs: Children of God; John 1:12, 8:41, Romans 8:14ff, Galatians 3:26, 4:6. God's peace; Philippians 4:4–7, 9. Wait patiently; Romans 8:24–26. His strength; 2 Thessalonians 3:3, Philippians 4:19. Wait on/hope in the Lord… Renew your strength; Judges 7, Isaiah 40:28–31. Apart from God you can do nothing; John 15:5. Christ who strengthens me; Philippians 4:13. Jesus is the vine, you are the branches; John 15. Enter God's rest; Hebrews 4:1–9. Whoever believes in me will do the works I have been doing and greater; John 14:1–14 (verse 12).

SHARE

1. Review the lesson and discuss the questions that are interesting to your group.

2. Is waiting in the presence of God easy, new, or a difficult concept for you? Explain.

3. If you consistently find strength in waiting on God, share your practical insights with the group.

4. Training with friends is always more fun than training alone. It is a proven fact that encouragement from others increases success. Commit to encouraging one another over the next six weeks. Practice 1 Thessalonians 5:11 and check in with each other at least twice a week for support.

> *Therefore encourage (admonish, exhort) one another and edify*
> *(strengthen and build up) one another, just as you are doing.*
> 1 Thessalonians 5:11 (AMP)

STRENGTH TRAINING
Your Time Alone With the Lord

GETTING STARTED:

Every day we need intentional time with the Lord. The next six weeks of our study together are designed to help you develop the intentional habit of looking to God for your strength and supply each day. Our prayer and expectation is that by establishing or reinforcing this habit you will:

*   Gain strength to face the ups and downs of each day.
*   You will grow in your understanding of God's love, power, and provision for your life.
*   You will grow in your ability to discern God's voice.
*   You will experience greater intimacy with the Lord.
*   You will fall deeper in love with Jesus than you ever imagined possible.

Daily Exercise: Practicing His Presence

Step One — Acknowledge

- Acknowledge God's presence is with you. Try saying, "Good Morning God! Thank you for being here with me!"

- Invite him into your day.

- As you go about your activities today practice waiting on God by intentionally redirecting your thoughts toward him throughout the day. Try setting the timer on your phone as a reminder.

> ### This Works for Me!
>
> "I'm a hairdresser. When I first started to practice his presence I bought blue dot stickers. I stuck them to some of my equipment in various places. When I came across them during the day they reminded me of the Holy Spirit's presence and power with me." —Pam

Step Two — Practice silence & solitude

Because we are so distracted with noise in this world, it is important to practice silence. Many people are addicted to the buzz whirling around us. Continual stimulation creates stress which zaps our strength. Practicing silence and solitude gives our hearts and minds a break and helps create space for us to HEAR from God.

If you've never done this before and you don't know how to live without your phone, TV, computer, or you can't stand the thought of being alone, take a deep breath! Set a timer for three minutes and try it. It will feel like an eternity, but do it anyway!

Choose a place comfortable for you.

When practicing silence and solitude do what is most comfortable for you. For example, grab some coffee and sit at the table or snuggle in your bed. Go for a walk in nature. Work in your garden. Shut the radio off in your car.

1. Choose location, time of day, and the length of time you will spend with the Lord (according to your schedule).

    Because we are each unique, we connect differently with the Lord. No two people connect in exactly the same way because our relationship with God is personal for each of us. We encourage you to consider and discover what works best for you.

2. To help you focus on his presence with you, choose a verse or passage from this week's lesson that speaks to your heart. Spend time talking with God about your need for strength in <u>one of the areas we've discussed</u>.

3. Write down your thoughts, feelings, mental pictures and impressions from your time with him.

    ARE YOU HAVING TROUBLE? If this is new for you, it may take a bit of time and patience to be able to settle yourself so you can sense the presence of the Lord with you. Don't be discouraged if you struggle. Choose one thought from the lesson or one of the verses to focus on. Read the thought or verse over and over; emphasize each phrase or word separately as you ask the Lord to speak to you through the words. If you are a writer, just start writing your thoughts, relying on the Lord to guide your words as they flow from your pen or the keys of your computer. Remember, this is for you alone. You won't be turning your thoughts over to anyone unless you choose to share at some point.

    IF YOU ARE AN EXPERIENCED OLD HAND AT THIS…enjoy every minute you can spare! If you really get excited, consider posting on the *STRONGER* Facebook page, or sending an email or text to the gals in your group to share a bit of your experience this week. Of course, this is optional, but *oh, so much fun!*

4. Throughout the day practice turning your thoughts to the Lord. Repeat the Scripture you chose and talk with him about your circumstances.

5. Practice praising him. Thank him for acting on your behalf in advance.

My Strength Training Journal

Keep track of what you learned this week. Take notes so you can share PRACTICAL *Strength Training* tips with your group.

What I learned about myself this week:

What I learned about God this week:

What I learned about *Strength Training* this week:

LEVEL 2: MOTION SICKNESS

FOCUS

BUSY – WEARY – WEAK

In the last session we learned that God is the source of our strength. In phase one of your *Strength Training* you took the first step of learning to wait. Why is waiting important? Because the Bible teaches that there is a connection between waiting on the Lord and gaining strength. (Isaiah 40:31 *...those who wait upon the Lord gain new strength*.) For many people learning to wait is challenging. We encouraged you to spend intentional time daily connecting with God in the way that works best for you.

Recap your progress with waiting on the Lord last week.

- How did you do?

- What worked best for you?

- What challenges did you face (i.e. distractions, interruptions, failure to plan, etc.)?

- What steps can you take this week to continue to build on your success from last week?

We have discovered that no matter how intentional we plan to be about our *Strength Training* time with God, something always competes for our attention. A lack of time is our biggest obstacle. We are constantly running from one activity to another. There are twenty four hours in a day and most of us wish we could squeeze a few more hours into our overscheduled lives. Why? Because our society confuses busyness with significance. How many times have you answered the question, "Hello, how are you?" with "Busy!"?

But beware! Busyness leads to weariness. The weary person lacks strength, focus, and peace. The dictionary defines weary as:

1. exhausted in strength, endurance, vigor, or freshness
2. having one's patience, tolerance, or pleasure exhausted

Have you ever experienced motion sickness? When I was young, my family took a few driving vacations. I loved to get to the final destination, but I hated the ride. Sitting in the back seat I felt every turn, every acceleration and deceleration. My pulse would race, I would begin to feel dizzy, and I would get nauseated and overheated. If I wasn't able to get out of that car and stop moving, everyone in the car would know just how rotten I was feeling. When our busy schedule creates weariness in our lives we have developed a type of spiritual motion sickness. The symptoms of spiritual motion sickness are obvious to ourselves and others. Symptoms may include exhaustion, staleness or apathy in relationship with God, hopelessness, impatience, intolerance, timidity, and fear.

Are you currently experiencing any symptoms of weariness such as exhaustion, impatience, intolerance, or fear?

Would you describe your life as busy? If so, what causes you to be busy? In the space below write down the activities in your typical day.

How much of your busy schedule is set aside to take care of your emotional, physical or spiritual well-being?

By the way, this guidebook is grace based. We are about grace not guilt, growth, not guilt! Don't feel bad about the pace of your life. Simply be aware. What can you do less to experience more of God?

> "I refer to weariness as *motion sickness*" —CJ Rapp

EXPLORE

Just looking at our list of to do's can cause us to feel weary. The truth is, there will always be something to do and someone who needs our attention. There is nothing wrong with being busy. The problem is how we are affected by our schedules. When busyness causes weariness-or motion sickness, our relationships with God and others suffer. Instead of responding in love and feeling peaceful, we begin to stress out and react. We become intolerant or impatient. We struggle to believe and have faith in adversity. Our flesh reacts with perhaps anger or frustration instead of responding with the spirit of Jesus within us. You can tell the difference. When we rest in the Lord and wait in his presence his Spirit grows strong within us. The fruit of the Spirit found in Galatians 5:22–23 then guides and governs our interactions, instead of our flesh.

> *But the fruit of the [Holy] Spirit [the work which His presence within accomplishes] is love, joy (gladness), peace, patience (an even temper, forbearance), kindness, goodness (benevolence), faithfulness, Gentleness (meekness, humility), self-control (self-restraint, countenance). Against such things there is no law [that can bring a charge].*
>
> Galatians 5:22–23 (AMP)

Just in case you think busyness is a twenty-first century problem that God doesn't know much about consider the life of Jesus. The book of Mark uses the word immediately no less than forty two times when describing the events of Jesus life and ministry. People demanded his time and their needs were great. We can all relate to feeling the stress of our responsibilities and caring for the needs of others who need our attention. For example:

- Mom is constantly bombarded with precious little hands needing her attention, perhaps a full time or part time job, ministry, PTA, carpool, and ministering to the needs of her home.

- The family man is constantly pulled in two directions; providing for the family and working those extra hours or spending time with his family.

- The student has on average six classes to study and prepare for, perhaps a part time job, chores, a social life, etc.

- Grandparents have to split their time between each child and their children.

In spite of a hurried life, Jesus protected his time alone with God often withdrawing to a place where he could be alone. In solitude he gained spiritual strength and direction. We never see Jesus suffering from signs of motion sickness. We never read of him barking at someone who needed healing, wondering if he

> *We must ruthlessly eliminate hurry from our lives.* —Dallas Willard

had the power to heal someone, fighting with the disciples, frustrated with yet another interruption or telling others to leave him alone. Jesus was just as busy if not more so than we are today. Yet he was intentional and protective about his time with his Father. He modeled for his disciples, both then and now, the importance of <u>intentional</u> time alone with God.

Mark 6 describes a series of events that teach us how important time alone with God is for us spiritually. Jesus called his disciples, gave them authority and power, and sent them out two by two to minister to the people and preach that men should repent. They were to go from city to city completely dependent upon him, his power, and provision for all their needs.

As you read the following passages, underline, highlight or note anything that stands out to you and make note of why this caught your attention. Consider sharing your thoughts with your group or a friend.

And He summoned the twelve and began to send them out in pairs, and gave them authority over the unclean spirits; and He instructed them that they should take nothing for their journey, except a mere staff—no bread, no bag, no money in their belt—but to wear sandals; and He added, "Do not put on two tunics." And He said to them, "Wherever you enter a house, stay there until you leave town. "Any place that does not receive you or listen to you, as you go out from there, shake the dust off the soles of your feet for a testimony against them." They went out and preached that men should repent. And they were casting out many demons and were anointing with oil many sick people and healing them.

Mark 6:7–13 (NASB)

*The apostles [sent out as missionaries] came back and
gathered together to Jesus, and told Him all that they had done
and taught. And He said to them, [As for you] come away by yourselves
to a deserted place, and rest a while—for many were [continually]
coming and going, and they had not even leisure enough to eat.
And they went away in a boat to a solitary place by themselves.*

Mark 6:30–32 (AMP)

While the disciples were away on their assignment Jesus received the news that his cousin, John, had been murdered by Herod (Mark 6:25–30). There is nothing that zaps our strength quite like loss. Jesus, being fully God and fully man, would have felt the pain of loss just like we do.

Imagine the excitement of the disciples over all they had experienced. They had cast out demons, healed the sick, seen men repent and who knows what else. The excitement of their experience had to spill outside into the streets because soon so many people were coming and going there was not even time to eat. I wonder if anyone stopped to ask Jesus how he was doing after the death of his cousin John. Jesus knew the disciples would soon crash from all their work. They needed to take care of themselves to prevent *motion sickness*. So he invited them to come away with him to a deserted place and rest. His invitation was and is simple:

- *Come away with me…* (NIV)

  Jesus' presence is the most important component of rest. His presence refreshes us.

- *…by yourselves* (NIV)

  Literally, "be alone with me." This is the discipline of solitude. If we are not alone we can easily be distracted by conversation, movement, or needs. Our focus on Jesus needs to be protected.

- *…to a secluded place* (NASB)

  A secluded place is free of distractions. Notice Jesus didn't say, let's go to the other room, or head over to Mark's house (or Starbuck's). The Greek definition of secluded is wilderness. The disciples didn't have the challenge of electronic leashes but they did have a house full of stuff and people. They didn't have TVs, computers, or Wi-Fi. In today's culture we must intentionally turn everything off to create a place of quietness.

- *...and rest a while* (AMP)

  What did this rest look like? It was free from the distractions of others. They left the house and went outside to a secluded place in nature.

How do you define the word rest?

How do you rest? Is there a place you like to go to rest, or something you like to do?

The Greek word *rest* means to become physically refreshed after a time of work. The dictionary defines rest as:

- Relief or freedom, especially from anything that wearies, troubles, or disturbs.
- A period or interval of inactivity, repose, solitude, or tranquility.
- Mental or spiritual calm.

To be clear, rest is NOT quiet time. Notice Jesus didn't say, get out your journals and your Bible and let's have quiet time. He said *come away with me* to a secluded place and rest. Think of it this way, rest—going away with Jesus—is refreshment for the soul. Quiet time renews the mind. Each are important and necessary for a vibrant relationship with the Lord. In today's church culture quiet time is the term most often used to describe our time with God. In it we get up early, read the Bible, write in our journals, pray, or read a devotional. When I ask people how their relationship with God is they often say, "Well I haven't been good about doing my quiet time." Relationship with God is not just a "to do" it's a "to be."

Jesus recognized the disciples need for rest even when they did not. As we all know, sometimes our best intentions to rest are thwarted by the "to do's" of life and the needs of others. We know the people saw Jesus and the disciples leave by boat and they ran ahead of them.

> *So they left by boat for a quiet place, where they could be alone. But many people recognized them and saw them leaving, and people from many towns ran ahead along the shore and got there ahead of them. Jesus saw the huge crowd as he stepped from the boat, and he had compassion on them because they were like sheep without a shepherd. So he began teaching them many things. Late in the afternoon his disciples came to him and said, "This is a remote place, and it's already getting late. Send the crowds away so they can go to the nearby farms and villages and buy something to eat." But Jesus said, "You feed them." "With what?" they asked. "We'd have to work for months to earn enough money to buy food for all these people!"*

Mark 6:32–37 (NLT)

In your opinion, what is wrong with the disciple's response to Jesus in verse 37? (Hint: review the symptoms of *motion sickness*.)

The disciple's response was, *"With what?"* It seems like a reasonable question. After all, the crowd is large, no one brought food, and they are all far from home. Are these not the same disciples who had just returned from a trip where they had experienced God's power at work through them? At what point did they shift from depending upon God to work through them to self-dependence? When busyness zapped their spiritual strength and they experienced motion sickness! Weariness takes our eyes off of Jesus as our provider. This is why we must practice rest! At some point, weakened by activity, we forget to lean on him for our supply.

CONTROL FREAK ALERT: This may be a difficult or overwhelming question, but can you describe a time in your life when you relied more on yourself and your resources than the Lord for provision, strength or power? It might be easier to recall a time when you relied on the Lord more than you relied on yourself. Use the chart on the next page to record your experiences.

A time when I leaned on God:	A time when I depended on myself:
How did this work for you?	How did this work for you?
What did I learn about God?	What did I learn about "me?"

Jesus instructed the disciples to gather the loaves and fishes. Then modeling dependence upon God and his provision, Jesus prayed. The five thousand were fed and there was more left over than they could eat. Jesus told the disciples to go ahead of him by boat as he dismissed the crowd. After everyone was gone he stopped to rest and pray.

The disciples, likely exhausted and completely empty, faced a new challenge...a storm.

> *And having seen that they were troubled and tormented in [their] rowing, for the wind was against them, about the fourth watch of the night [between 3:00–6:00 a.m.] He came to them, walking [directly] on the sea. And He acted as if He meant to pass by them, But when they saw Him walking on the sea they thought it was a ghost, and raised a [deep, throaty] shriek of terror. For they all saw Him and were agitated (troubled and filled with fear and dread). But immediately He talked with them and said, Take heart! I AM! Stop being alarmed and afraid. And He went up into the boat with them, and the wind ceased (sank to rest as if exhausted by its own beating). And they were astonished exceedingly [beyond measure],*
> *For they failed to consider or understand [the teaching and meaning of the miracle of] the loaves; [in fact] their hearts had grown callous*
> *[had become dull and had lost the power of understanding].*
>
> Mark 6:48–52 (AMP)

Not only does weariness cause motion sickness, but it also prevents us from recognizing Jesus in our circumstances. When we do not take time to rest and refresh we become dull and lose the power of spiritual understanding allowing our emotions to get the better of us.

Jesus invites us to rest with him. And when we have pushed our limits he doesn't scold us, he loves us. His invitation is sweet, loving and ongoing.

> *Come to Me, all you who labor and are heavy-laden and overburdened, and I will*
> *cause you to rest. [I will ease and relieve and refresh your souls.] Take My yoke*
> *upon you and learn of Me, for I am gentle (meek) and humble (lowly) in heart,*
> *and you will find rest (relief and ease and refreshment and recreation and blessed*
> *quiet) for your souls. For My yoke is wholesome (useful, good—not harsh, hard,*
> *sharp, or pressing, but comfortable, gracious, and pleasant), and*
> *My burden is light and easy to be borne.*
>
> Matthew 11:28–30 (AMP)

Come to me is a present tense invitation issued again each day. The rest he provides refreshes body, soul, and spirit supplying what you need for this day, just like the manna he provided in the desert.

LEARNING TO REST

Rest must be built into the rhythm of our lives. The strength for today is not fueled by yesterday's rest. Even muscles, as they are being worked and built-up, need a time of rest and recovery in order for them to grow and become strong. Intentional time with the Lord is our goal. For those of you who experience guilt when you sit to rest, we give you permission to rest. You matter. Taking time to rest is not selfish. In fact, it is the best thing you can do for those you love. Rest results in the ability to interact with others out of the overflow of your time with God instead of your worn-out flesh. Rest also changes your perspective, allowing you to see others and circumstances from God's point of view.

For some people, developing the habit of resting with Jesus can be hard to define and put into action. This simple acrostic will help you get started.

R = RELAX

Take a break and breathe.

> *The time came when the Lord God formed a man's body*
> *from the dust of the ground and breathed into it the breath of life.*
> *And man became a living person.*

Genesis 2:7 (TLB)

God breathed into Adam and before Jesus ascended into heaven he breathed on the disciples and said receive the Holy Spirit. There must be something important here! Think of breathing in his presence, power and strength and with every exhale cleansing the junk that weighs us down. Actually taking long deep breaths has a calming effect on our physical body and our emotions. As we breathe, our heart rate slows and stress and tension are released. Intentionally breathe this way until you feel relaxed.

Most likely, the minute you start to relax, your mind will be flooded with a list of "to do's." These distractions are your enemy coming up to rob you of peace. Simply arm yourself with a notepad to write down every "need to do" that comes to your mind. Eventually the busyness of your brain will slow down. Remember, the enemy loves to use distraction to keep us from spending quality time with the Lord. The process of learning to relax may be the most challenging part of rest. As you work at this intentional relaxation exercise it will become easier and faster. Stay with it! You will be so glad you persevered.

E = ENTER IN

How do you enter into his presence?

As you relax, your mind clears and you are able to intentionally focus on him. It is important to remember Jesus tells us ...*surely I am with you always, to the very end of the age* (Matthew 28:20 NIV). We never have to conjure him up. We only need to become aware of his presence with us. We can simply say aloud, "thank you for being here with me." Faith comes by hearing, so saying this aloud strengthens your awareness of his presence and your faith.

Next praise him for whatever comes to your mind.

> *Enter into His gates with thanksgiving and a thank offering and into His courts*
> *with praise! Be thankful and say so to Him, bless and affectionately praise His*
> *name! For the Lord is good; His mercy and loving-kindness are everlasting, His*
> *faithfulness and truth endure to all generations.*

Psalm 100:4–5 (AMP)

Why? Psalm 22:3 tells us God inhabits the praises of his people. Thank him for everything you can think of, especially his presence. As we focus on the sufficiency and faithfulness of God, the "to do's" and worries of the day slip away. The realization of all he has done for us reminds us of his goodness.

S = STEEP

Steep means to:

- soak in water or other liquid, as to soften, cleanse, or extract some element or component

- wet thoroughly in or with a liquid; drench; saturate; imbue (impregnate or inspire)

- immerse in or saturate or imbue with some pervading, absorbing, astounding or amazing influence or agency

When you place a tea bag in a glass of hot water, what happens? The water changes to tea. The longer we immerse or soak in the presence of God the more we are infused with his character and love. As we steep, we don't have to say anything. We can just be still and enjoy being with him. We hear him best when we are not talking!

Be still and know that I am God!
Psalm 46:10a (NLT)

T = TALK WITH

Communication is an essential element of relationships. In fact no one has ever had a successful relationship without communication. Talking together is the way we get to know one another. One of the greatest misconceptions about God is that we cannot have a conversation with him. We end up talking at God instead of talking with God. The Bible teaches us how God relates to us; throughout the Bible he speaks to people. The Lord spoke with Moses face to face as a man speaks with his friend (Exodus 33:11). David poured his heart out to God and had conversations with him recorded in Psalms. Jesus spoke with Paul and the disciples AFTER his death and resurrection. HE values relationships. He wants to talk with us about the things on our hearts—our hopes, dreams, families—everything. He wants to tell us he loves us and is for us. But we must listen and not just talk.

Perhaps the most important words ever spoken in regard to our ongoing relationship with Jesus were:

> *The sheep that are My own hear and are listening to My voice;*
> *and I know them, and they follow Me.*

John 10:27 (AMP)

Practice talking *with* God. Talk and LISTEN. Share your thoughts with him and then listen to his response. Don't dismiss the still small voice. Listen for great ideas, record pictures that pop into your mind or feelings that wash over you. Do dismiss any voice that is accusatory, condemning, or condescending. Consider writing your conversation down. Use a black or blue pen for your words and a red pen for God's words. Listen with anticipation. Try to plan so you won't be in a rush—Jesus is not on your time schedule. You will likely begin with short commitments to your time with him; but as you develop your ability to hear him, you will long for more time.

GOD'S HEART FOR YOU

You are my precious child and nothing pleases me more than to hear you entering into my presence. Come to me as if turning around and seeing me with my arms wide open to receive you. I am that close to you and that eager to hold you close to my heart. I call you to REST in me continually. I see you struggle with restlessness and uncertainty; this is far from what I desire for you. I desire for you to remain in me and in my love. Remove any distractions that keep you too busy to sit and relax with me. Enter into my presence… come away with me, just the two of us. Seek me when you don't sense me near. Listen for my voice; I am speaking, but you must listen more than you speak if you desire to hear me. Trust that you can hear my voice. Trust that I will speak and give you discernment. I will withhold no good thing from you. I want you to know my voice; just as the sheep know their shepherd's voice, you can know my voice.

In my presence you will find true REST and refreshment. I will fully equip you for all that lies before you. Do not fear or doubt; I will teach you to know my voice. Come into my presence…I am waiting for you.

~~~~~~~~~~~

God's presence; Psalm 73:28. Seek God; 2 Chronicles 15:2, Psalm 9:10, 27:4, 53:2, Proverbs 8:17, Isaiah 55:6, Jeremiah 29:13. Remain in me and in my love; John 15:4, 9–10, 22. He hears my voice; John: 10:27. Trust that God hears your voice; 2 Samuel 22:7, Psalm 5:3, Psalm 55:17, Psalm 116:1. God will meet all your needs; Philippians 4:19. Fear not; Isaiah 41:10.

SHARE

1. Review the lesson and discuss questions that are interesting to your group.

2. If you haven't already, share your experience regarding your time spent with the Lord. What obstacles did you face and how you will handle them this week?

3. If you feel comfortable, share how you felt as you left your time with God (weird/refreshed/embarrassed, etc.). Were you able to continue your connection with God into the rest of your day? Remember, you or someone in your group may be starting a new chapter in walking with the Lord and it will be a growing process.

4. Training with friends is always more fun than training alone. If you haven't established a training partner yet, be sure to do that before you leave the group today. For this study we recommend you connect with one or two buddies. Commit to sharing with one another over the remainder of this study together. Practice 1 Thessalonians 5:11 and encourage each other at least once a week.

*Therefore encourage (admonish, exhort) one another and edify
(strengthen and build up) one another, just as you are doing.*

1 Thessalonians 5:11 (AMP)

STRENGTH TRAINING
INCORPORATING REST

GETTING STARTED:

Every day we need intentional time with the Lord. Our study together is designed to help you develop the intentional habit of looking to God for your strength and supply each day.

This week we learned the importance of REST. Let's make this personal. Remember the definition of rest is refreshment after a time of work. What makes rest refreshing is practicing the presence of Jesus, which we learned last week. The practice of REST should refresh the body, mind, and spirit. Because we are uniquely created, we need to explore what type of rest refreshes us. Rest should be practiced daily, weekly, quarterly, and yearly. In the exercise below list what refreshes you. Give this some thought. Don't spiritualize it—if you like going for a walk, sewing, gardening, etc. write it down.

What Refreshes Me?

Yearly!_____

Quarterly!_____

Weekly!_____

Daily!_____

Doing what refreshes us **+** practicing the presence of God **=** REST.

Your goal this week is:

- Practice daily refreshment.
- Practice your weekly refreshment.

Daily Exercise: Practicing Rest

Do what refreshes you daily while practicing his presence.

Step One — Do What You Enjoy!

Remember to incorporate REST while doing what you enjoy.

R = Relax

E = Enter in

S = Steep

T = Talk with

This Works for Me!

I love to go for daily hikes. It clears my mind and reduces stress. I love the idea of practicing REST while hiking. I relax and enter into his presence by enjoying my surroundings and thanking him for the beauty of nature. I can steep in him just by taking in all he created. While I walk, I talk and listen. Sometimes I feel as if he is answering me through the birds singing or the sun warming me. —CJ

Step Two — Record What You Learned

Make sure you record what you learned, felt, or heard in your *Strength Training Journal*.

Do you feel rested?

WEEKLY EXERCISE: PRACTICING REST

Do what refreshes you weekly while practicing God's presence.

STEP ONE — DO WHAT YOU LOVE TO DO TO FEEL REFRESHED

Remember to incorporate REST while doing what you enjoy.

R = Relax

E = Enter in

S = Steep

T = Talk with

STEP TWO — RECORD WHAT YOU LEARNED

Make sure you record what you learned, felt, or heard in your *Strength Training Journal*.

Do you feel rested?

Finally, don't feel guilty if you can't do this daily or practice the once a week rest. But be AWARE. What obstacles came up? What is your plan to overcome the distractions next week? Make sure to write your plan down in your journal.

My Strength Training Journal

Keep track of what you learned this week. Take notes so you can share PRACTICAL *Strength Training* tips with your group.

What I learned about myself this week:

What I learned about God this week:

What I learned about *Strength Training* this week:

Come with me
by yourselves
to a quiet place
and get some

REST.

Mark 6:31 (NIV)

LEVEL 3: IDENTIFYING HEART DIS-EASE, PART 1

FOCUS

Last week we learned how important it is to REST. In God's presence we are able to slow down, gain a fresh perspective, be encouraged and renew our strength. Without intentional time alone with the Lord we experience motion sickness. Our fast paced busy lives cause us to become weary, worn out, freaked out, and stressed out. Our physical, emotional and spiritual strength is drained and our flesh begins to react instead of respond to the ups and downs of life. Strength training is really about learning to *REST in* and *seek after* God's presence as our vital need.

For review, what does it mean to REST?

R = _____.

E = _____.

S = _____.

T = _____.

On a scale of 1 to 10, how successful were you at your daily *Strength Training* exercise this past week?

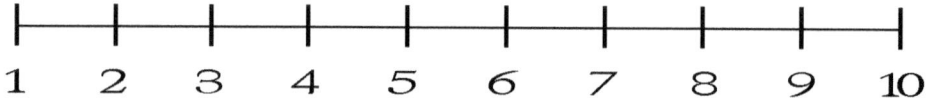

1   2   3   4   5   6   7   8   9   10

What happened that distracted you from your time with the Lord?

How can you avoid distractions this week?

What did REST look like for you last week (i.e. hiking, gardening, painting, etc.)?

How did you feel as you practiced REST? Circle all that apply in the cloud below.

Joyful   Itchy
Distracted
Anxious   Confused
Relaxed *Awkward*   Nervous
Hurried   Overwhelmed
Nothing   Peaceful
Other_____

What, if anything, did you learn about yourself?

What, if anything, did you learn about God?

How did your time with him affect the rest of your day?

Practicing the presence of God takes discipline. Learning to be alone in quiet with him is a key discipline for spiritual growth.

Remember REST is not the absence of activity, though it certainly
can be. It is doing what refreshes you plus practicing awareness of his
presence with you that equals rest.

EXPLORE

In Matthew 11:28–30, Jesus invited all those who were, and are today, weary and heavy-laden to:

> *Come to Me, all you who labor and are heavy-laden and overburdened, and I will*
> *cause you to rest. [I will ease and relieve and refresh your souls.] Take My yoke upon*
> *you and learn of Me, for I am gentle (meek) and humble (lowly) in heart,*
> *and you will find rest (relief and ease and refreshment and recreation and blessed*
> *quiet) for your souls. For My yoke is wholesome (useful, good—not harsh, hard,*
> *sharp, or pressing, but comfortable, gracious, and pleasant),*
> *and My burden is light and easy to be borne.*
> Matthew 11:28–30 (AMP)

Perhaps the sweetest of all invitations is simply *come to me*. Jesus invites us to come close and lean on him. He desires for us to feel comfortable and free to bring him the concerns we carry and the burdens that weigh us down. Imagine drawing near to him, laying your head upon his shoulder and telling him of your struggles, hurts, and fears – anything that causes weariness. *Come to me* is an invitation to intimacy.

*Come to me…*is followed by *learn of me. Learn of me…*in other words, get to know me. Spend time with me by yoking yourself to me. Jesus then describes himself as *gentle and humble in heart*. Jesus promises we will experience rest and refreshment in his presence.

Why do you think Jesus described himself as gentle and humble in heart?

Give an example of what gentle and humble in heart looks like in actions or attitude.

We think gentle and humble in heart are significant because it makes him approachable. To be peaceful and able to rest in the presence of Jesus, one would have to know with certainty they are accepted by him.

If you've never had the experience of *being with* Jesus and only know *of him* it might not ever occur to you to approach him intimately. You may feel uncertainty about how he would react and what he would say about the choices you've made that created weariness and burdens. Because he is gentle (mild and kind in temperament, courteous, and noble) and humble in heart (not condescending) we can feel safe coming to him.

Perhaps Jesus described himself as humble and gentle so people would not fear him, but be drawn to him. After years of ministry one consistent theme has become clear; people in general have misconceptions about who he is and how he sees them. Instead of drawing near and finding the comfort, rest, refreshment, acceptance and love that is available, many pull back. They experience *heart dis-ease* when they think about being in relationship with the Lord. This makes it difficult to develop the personal intimate relationship he offers.

WHAT IS *HEART DIS-EASE*?

Heart dis-ease is a condition rooted in fear caused by a misconception about who God is, how God sees you and how he relates to you. It prevents a person from drawing near and being able to experience the love, comfort, rest, refreshment, acceptance and peace that comes from intimacy with God.

DO WE NEED A HEART CHECK?

The heart is the center of our thoughts, emotions and will. When we feel *heart dis-ease,* we need to investigate why because Proverbs 4:23 says, *Guard your heart more than anything else, because the source of your life flows from it* (GW).

When we avoid time with him, feel itchy, uncomfortable, fearful, or experience any negative feelings about spending time with the Lord, it is time we perform a heart check.

HEART CHECK:

We need to check in with our heart and ask, what is going on? What is preventing me from coming to and being comfortable in his presence? What do I believe about who God is or how he sees me that makes me feel uncomfortable in his presence?

When we have an inaccurate picture of who God is and how he relates to us, we are unable to come to him without apprehension and dis-ease. One of the most telling signs of *heart dis-ease* is restlessness in his presence. This is why we must continually be aware of our thoughts and attitudes toward God and how we feel about the time we spend with him.

To perform a heart check, I need to understand where *my view of God* comes from.

Ask:

- Where did my view of God come from?

- Who taught me about God first?

- How did I learn about God, Jesus, and the Holy Spirit?

- How did I develop my idea of who God is?

- How is my view of God continuing to grow?

- What experiences have I had with God that are personal and intimate and have helped me to form an opinion about who God is, how he sees me, and how he interacts with me?

- Because the Bible describes God in relational terms, are any of my earthly relationships affecting the way I relate to or interact with him?

WHERE MY VIEW OF GOD COMES FROM

Our personal understanding of who God is and how he relates to us comes from our personal experience and our relationships.

PERSONAL EXPERIENCE

After becoming followers of Jesus, we learn the core spiritual disciplines of the Christian life, which include:

READING THE BIBLE, WHICH TEACHES US:

- Who God is

- Who we are in his sight

- How he relates to us

- How he wants us to live

However, we don't always learn study skills that help us accurately observe, interpret, and apply what the Bible says to our lives.

PRAYING (HABITS AND PRACTICES)

- Learning to pray about everything
- Reading Scriptures about how God hears and answers our prayers

Two of the most well-known verses about prayer are:

> *Ask, and it will be given to you; seek, and you will find; knock, and it will be opened to you. For everyone who asks receives, and he who seeks finds, and to him who knocks it will be opened.*
>
> Matthew 7:7–8 (NASB)

> *…You do not have because you do not ask.*
>
> James 4:2b (NASB)

When we base our prayer life on verses like these without understanding the context (what comes before and what comes after these passages) we are setting ourselves up for disappointment and *heart dis-ease.*

Why? Because lifting verses and principals out of the Bible without context creates misunderstanding of the intended meaning and, consequently, incorrect application.

This, in turn, creates unrealistic expectations of God, leading to disappointment and *heart dis-ease.*

Unfortunately, over the years we have encountered many people who asked God for something they truly believed was a good thing. They believed God would give it to them only to become completely discouraged, disappointed, disillusioned and sometimes angry at God because he failed to answer their prayer according to their expectations.

After all, praying for healing, the restoration of marriage, a job, that someone wouldn't die, a good grade on a final, or not to lose a home is not self-serving prayer, right? What happens when you believe you are asking for a good thing and it doesn't happen? Many people get angry with God and are so disappointed and disillusioned they stop talking to him altogether. They actually hold it against him. It is very difficult to reconcile the goodness of God with our disappointment in God and that is when offense happens.

When the offended person harbors unforgiveness toward God, he or she may find it difficult if not impossible, to practice the presence of the Lord. Unforgiveness causes restlessness and limits our ability to REST in his presence.

> *To be offended is to take offense at someone's character, words, or conduct so as to reject him.*

In order to prevent *heart dis-ease* caused by unmet expectations, we must be completely honest with God, and ourselves, just as David was in the Psalms. David had perhaps the most intimate relationship with God of any human being except John, *The Beloved Disciple*. David knew what it was to be disappointed by an unanswered prayer.

In Second Samuel we learn King David had an affair with a woman named Bathsheba. She was the wife of one of David's fighting men named Uriah. While Uriah was away in battle, Bathsheba became pregnant with David's child. David went to great lengths to hide his sin. He even called Uriah back from the battle lines with the hope he would be intimate with Bathsheba and believe the baby was his. However, Uriah was an honorable man and because his men had no such opportunity to be with their wives he refused to enjoy his wife. He returned to the battlefront where David had him killed. David then took Bathsheba as his wife believing no one would know about their indiscretion. But God knew.

> *"Indeed you did it secretly, but I will do this thing before all Israel, and under the sun." Then David said to Nathan, "I have sinned against the LORD." And Nathan said to David, "The LORD also has taken away your sin; you shall not die. "However, because by this deed you have given occasion to the enemies of the LORD to blaspheme, the child also that is born to you shall surely die." So Nathan went to his house. Then the LORD struck the child that Uriah's widow bore to David, so that he was very sick. David therefore inquired of God for the child; and David fasted and went and lay all night on the ground. The elders of his household stood beside him in order to raise him up from the ground, but he was unwilling and would not eat food with them. Then it happened on the seventh day*

that the child died. And the servants of David were afraid to tell him that the child was dead, for they said, "Behold, while the child was still alive, we spoke to him and he did not listen to our voice. How then can we tell him that the child is dead, since he might do himself harm!" But when David saw that his servants were whispering together, David perceived that the child was dead; so David said to his servants, "Is the child dead?" And they said, "He is dead." So David arose from the ground, washed, anointed himself, and changed his clothes; and he came into the house of the LORD and worshiped. Then he came to his own house, and when he requested, they set food before him and he ate. Then his servants said to him, "What is this thing that you have done? While the child was alive, you fasted and wept; but when the child died, you arose and ate food." He said, "While the child was still alive, I fasted and wept; for I said, 'Who knows, the LORD may be gracious to me, that the child may live.' "But now he has died; why should I fast? Can I bring him back again? I will go to him, but he will not return to me."

2 Samuel 12:12–23 (NASB)

David prayed, he petitioned, he believed, and when God didn't respond as David requested, he accepted God's will and moved on. After this experience David wrote Psalm 51, which expressed his true heart before God.

Have mercy on me, O God, according to your unfailing love; according to your great compassion blot out my transgressions. Wash away all my iniquity and cleanse me from my sin. For I know my transgressions, and my sin is always before me. Against you, you only, have I sinned and done what is evil in your sight; so you are right in your verdict and justified when you judge. Surely I was sinful at birth, sinful from the time my mother conceived me. Yet you desired faithfulness even in the womb; you taught me wisdom in that secret place. Cleanse me with hyssop, and I will be clean; wash me, and I will be whiter than snow. Let me hear joy and gladness; let the bones you have crushed rejoice. Hide your face from my sins and blot out all my iniquity. Create in me a pure heart, O God, and renew a steadfast spirit within me. Do not cast me from your presence or take your Holy Spirit from me. Restore to me the joy of your salvation and grant me a willing spirit, to sustain me. Then I will teach transgressors your ways, so that sinners will turn back to you. Deliver me from the guilt of bloodshed, O God, you who are God my Savior, and my tongue will sing of your righteousness. Open my lips, Lord, and my mouth will

> *declare your praise. You do not delight in sacrifice, or I would bring it; you do not take pleasure in burnt offerings. My sacrifice, O God, is a broken spirit; a broken and contrite heart you, God, will not despise.*
>
> Psalm 51:1–17 (NIV)

David could have allowed his disappointment and pain to separate him from the Lord. Instead, David chose to lean in, to worship, and to recognize God's sovereignty.

To prevent offense, I need to manage my expectations of God by dying to outcome management.

Like David, when you are disappointed, go to the Lord and tell him. When you are sad tell him. When you are mad at him, tell him. Intimacy is being able to be completely honest and transparent with someone. God already knows how you feel. Your relationship with him deepens when you talk with him about what is really going on in your heart and mind. Don't be afraid, don't hold back.

God is big enough to handle your anger, disappointment, resentment, frustration, and sadness. Tell him the truth and tell him you forgive him. Tell him you understand he is God and you are not. Tell him you still love him and ask for help to overcome any doubts you have about his goodness and love for you.

Have you prayed and been disappointed or even angered at God's response or perceived lack thereof? What did you ask for? What happened?

How did your unanswered prayer affect your relationship with and trust in God? Are you/were you tempted to believe God loves you less than he loves someone else? Explain your answer.

What, if anything, can you praise God for in the circumstance you described above?

Our Relationships

GOD IS RELATIONAL

We are part of his family. He describes himself in family terms, Father, Son, and Holy Spirit, to help us understand who he is and how to relate to him. We forget our relationships are flawed because we are human and imperfect. The problem we face is our assumption that God relates to us as people relate to one another. The truth is that God's character, his very nature, is not human.

GOD IS OUR FATHER

STOP – think of your earthly dad. Can you picture his face? Can you hear his voice? When you hear God is called your father, do you relate your earthly father's voice, mannerisms, expressions, temperament, actions, and attitude to God? The word father naturally causes us to think of our relationship with our dad. When we try to understand God as our father it is natural to impose the qualities and characteristics of our earthly father, good or bad, on to God. We face difficulty in our relationship with God if we view him through the grid of our relational experience with our dads.

Do you suddenly hear your father's voice instead of God the Father's? If so, this is called *relationship replay.*

Relationship replay happens when we associate in memory or imagination, the character of your dad with the character of God.

Prayerfully and honestly work through the following exercise and questions. You will not be asked to share your answers. Take your time.

Circle the characteristics that most remind you of your earthly father:

Unloving   Fun
Absent
Strong   *Always there*
Harsh   Critical
Gentle   Protective
Doting   **Negative**   Preoccupied
Angry   Abusive   Hard to please
Demanding   *Supportive*
Kind
Loving   Mean

Circle the words that describe how your earthly father made/makes you feel.

Significant   Loved
Rejected   *Ashamed*
Adored   *Beautiful*   *Valuable*
Unloved   **Encouraged**   Secure
Unwanted   *Safe*   *Apprehensive*
Worthless   Insignificant
Important   Abandoned
Insecure   *Self Conscious*

How is God like your earthly father? Explain.

Note the wording of the question "How is God like your earthly father?" To prevent *heart dis-ease* we must understand, once and for all, God is NOT like your earthly father. To say God is like our father is to make God over in the image of man. Man is fallen, imperfect and sinful. God is holy, perfect, and pure. In fact, God is love. Love is his character.

Beware...

Character association can lead to character assignation!

Whether your father was a *Leave it to Beaver, Brady Bunch,* or *Andy Griffith* kind of a dad, or an absent, abusive, or somewhere in the middle kind of dad, is irrelevant. God is different—he is a perfect father; you can enjoy a very different relationship with him.

> *Therefore you are to be perfect, as your heavenly Father is perfect.*
> Matthew 5:48 (NASB)

WHAT MAKES GOD A PERFECT FATHER?

He is an involved father from your conception!

> *...You formed my inward parts; You wove me in my mother's womb. I will give thanks to You, for I am fearfully and wonderfully made; Wonderful are Your works, And my soul knows it very well. My frame was not hidden from You, When I was made in secret, And skillfully wrought in the depths of the earth; Your eyes have seen my unformed substance; And in Your book were all written the days that were ordained for me, When as yet there was not one of them.*
> Psalm 139:13–16 (NASB)

♥ Because God is involved from my conception I can feel confident and secure.

He is a father who loves you as much as he loves Jesus.

> *I in them and you in me. May they be brought to complete unity to let the world know that you sent me and have loved them even as you have loved me.*
>
> John 17:23 (NIV)

♥ Because God loves me as much as he loves Jesus I can feel loved.

He is a father who is gracious and compassionate, not distant or angry.

> *The Lord is gracious and full of compassion, slow to anger and abounding in mercy and loving-kindness. The Lord is good to all, and His tender mercies are over all His works [the entirety of things created].*
>
> Psalm 145:8–9 (AMP)

♥ Because God is a father who is gracious and compassionate not distant or angry I can feel confident.

He is a father who lavishes you with love and calls you his child.

> *See how very much our Father loves us, for he calls us his children, and that is what we are! But the people who belong to this world don't recognize that we are God's children because they don't know him.*
>
> 1 John 3:1 (NLT)

♥ Because he lavishes his children with love I have a healthy identity and a sense of belonging.

He is a provider who meets your every need.

> *So don't worry about these things, saying, "What will we eat? What will we drink?*
> *What will we wear?" These things dominate the thoughts of unbelievers, but your*
> *heavenly Father already knows all your needs. Seek the Kingdom of God*
> *above all else, and live righteously, and he will give you everything you need. So*
> *don't worry about tomorrow, for tomorrow will bring its own worries.*
> *Today's trouble is enough for today.*
>
> Matthew 6:31–34 (NLT)

♥ Because my needs are provided for I can feel secure.

He protects his children.

> *Say this: "GOD, you're my refuge. I trust in you and I'm safe!"*
> *That's right—he rescues you from hidden traps, shields you*
> *from deadly hazards. His huge outstretched arms protect you—under*
> *them you're perfectly safe; his arms fend off all harm.*
>
> Psalm 91:2–4 (The Message)

♥ Because he is my refuge I can feel safe and protected.

If you experience restlessness in his presence it could be that you have an inaccurate understanding of your Heavenly Father and his love for you. Spend a few minutes asking the Lord to reveal to you any misgivings you have about him as your father. Write down any impression, memory or feeling that comes to mind.

Ask the Lord to give you a new, personal experience with him as your father. Ask him to take away any feelings of anger, resentment or unforgiveness that block you from experiencing intimacy with him. (Don't forget your part: let it go! This is for your benefit, not his.)

Wrapping It Up

Because the Godhead is personal and we enjoy a relationship with each member, it is important to know the roles and character of each. God is unchanging. Each member of the trinity functions personally in our lives. All their interactions are guided by love, faithfulness, and gentleness.

The Bible is written not just to tell us about God but to demonstrate how he relates to us. The Scripture refers to Jesus as our sibling, husband, and friend. However, he is not like any person you are, or ever have been, in relationship with. The same is true of the Holy Spirit who is our comforter and helper. Each member of the Godhead is uniquely for you. Each loves you with an everlasting love. Cultivate a relationship with each member. Ask him to show you if your earthly relationships have limited your relationship with him in any way. Do this so you will set your heart at ease in his presence. You will be able to REST comfortably in the completely loving and trustworthy arms of the one who loves you perfectly.

God's Heart for You

See the *Father's Love Letter* on the next page.

Father's Love Letter is a compilation of the following paraphrased Bible verses presented in the form of a love letter from God to you... (1) Psalm 139:1; (2) Psalm 139:2; (3) Psalm 139:3; (4) Matthew 10:29–31; (5) Genesis 1:27; (6) Acts 17:28; (7) Jeremiah 1:4–5; (8) Ephesians 1:11–12; (9) Psalm 139:15–16; (10) Acts 17:26; (11) Psalm 139:14; (12) Psalm 139:13; (13) Psalm 71:6; (14) John 8:41–44; (15) 1 John 4:16; (16) 1 John 3:1; (17) Matthew 7:11; (18) Matthew 5:48; (19) James 1:17; (20) Matthew 6:31–33; (21) Jeremiah 29:11; (22) Jeremiah 31:3; (23) Psalm 139:17–18; (24) Zephaniah 3:17; (25) Jeremiah 32:40; (26) Exodus 19:5; (27) Jeremiah 32:41; (28) Jeremiah 33:3; (29) Deuteronomy 4:29; (30) Psalm 37:4; (31) Philippians 2:13; (32) Ephesians 3:20; (33) 2 Thessalonians 2:16–17; (34) 2 Corinthians 1:3–4; (35) Psalm 34:18; (36) Isaiah 40:11; (37) Revelation 21:3–4; (38) John 17:23; (39) John 17:26; (40) Hebrews 1:3; (41) Romans 8:31; (42) 2 Corinthians 5:18–19; (43) 1 John 4:10; (44) Romans 8:31–32; (45) 1 John 2:23; (46) Romans 8:38–39 (47) Luke 15:7; (48) Ephesians 3:14–15; (49) John 1:12–13; (50) Luke 15:11–32. © 1999 Father Heart Communications FathersLoveLetter.com—Please feel free to copy & share with others.

FATHER'S LOVE LETTER

An intimate message from God to you.

My Child,

You may not know me, but I know everything about you.[1] I know when you sit down and when you rise up.[2] I am familiar with all your ways.[3] Even the very hairs on your head are numbered.[4] For you were made in my image.[5] In me you live and move and have your being, for you are my offspring.[6] I knew you even before you were conceived.[7] I chose you when I planned creation.[8] You were not a mistake, for all your days are written in my book.[9] I determined the exact time of your birth and where you would live.[10] You are fearfully and wonderfully made.[11] I knit you together in your mother's womb.[12] And brought you forth on the day you were born.[13] I have been misrepresented by those who don't know me.[14] I am not distant and angry, but am the complete expression of love.[15] And it is my desire to lavish my love on you. Simply because you are my child and I am your Father.[16] I offer you more than your earthly father ever could.[17] For I am the perfect father.[18] Every good gift that you receive comes from my hand.[19] For I am your provider and I meet all your needs.[20] My plan for your future has always been filled with hope.[21] Because I love you with an everlasting love.[22] My thoughts toward you are countless as the sand on the seashore.[23] And I rejoice over you with singing.[24] I will never stop doing good to you.[25] For you are my treasured possession.[26] I desire to establish you with all my heart and all my soul.[27] And I want to show you great and marvelous things.[28] If you seek me with all your heart, you will find me.[29] Delight in me and I will give you the desires of your heart.[30] For it is I who gave you those desires.[31] I am able to do more for you than you could possibly imagine.[32] For I am your greatest encourager.[33] I am also the Father who comforts you in all your troubles.[34] When you are brokenhearted, I am close to you.[35] As a shepherd carries a lamb, I have carried you close to my heart.[36] One day I will wipe away every tear from your eyes. And I'll take away all the pain you have suffered on this earth.[37] I am your Father, and I love you even as I love my son, Jesus.[38] For in Jesus, my love for you is revealed.[39] He is the exact representation of my being.[40] He came to demonstrate that I am for you, not against you.[41] And to tell you that I am not counting your sins. Jesus died so that you and I could be reconciled.[42] His death was the ultimate expression of my love for you. [43] I gave up everything I loved that I might gain your love.[44] If you receive the gift of my son Jesus, you receive me.[45] And nothing will ever separate you from my love again.[46] Come home and I'll throw the biggest party heaven has ever seen.[47] I have always been Father, and will always be Father.[48] My question is… Will you be my child?[49] I am waiting for you.[50]

Love, Your Dad
...Almighty God

SHARE

1. Review the lesson and discuss the questions that are interesting to your group.

2. If you haven't already, share your experience with your attempts to spend time with the Lord.

3. If you feel comfortable, share how you felt as you left your time with God. Were you able to carry your connection with him into the rest of your day or for a little while? Remember, you may be starting a new chapter of your walk with the Lord and it will be a growing process.

4. Training with friends is always more fun than training alone. If you haven't established a training buddy yet, be sure to do that before you leave today. Commit to encouraging one another over the remainder of this study together. Practice 1 Thessalonians 5:11 and check-in with each other at least twice a week for support.

> *Therefore encourage (admonish, exhort) one another and edify*
> *(strengthen and build up) one another, just as you are doing.*
>
> 1 Thessalonians 5:11 (AMP)

STRENGTH TRAINING

GETTING STARTED:

This week we learned to identify the causes of *heart dis-ease*. For your *Strength Training* exercise, practice combining the presence of God with the daily rest exercise that refreshes you, be aware of your thoughts and feelings. Remember we want to identify and stamp out *heart dis-ease* as it impacts our ability to be completely at ease with the Lord. If you discover that you are experiencing a feeling of restlessness, anxiety, fear, or shame. STOP and SEARCH for the root cause.

HEART CHECK:

The questions below will help you discover what shaped your view of God and how he relates to you. Answer thoughtfully. Ask the Lord to show you any misconceptions that could lead to *heart dis-ease* in his presence.

- Who first taught you about God the Father? Jesus? Holy Spirit? And when?

- What were you told about each of them?
  - o Describe in detail what you believe God the Father is like. What does your relationship with the Father look like? Are you tempted to apply the same characteristics to Father God that your dad had? Which ones? How does that strengthen or weaken your relationship with Father God (for example, do they draw you near, or cause you to step back from intimacy)?

  - o Describe in detail what you believe Jesus is like and your relationship with him. In the Bible, Jesus is called our friend, sibling, and bridegroom. Picture in your mind your brother, sister, friends, and spouse. Are you tempted to apply the same characteristics to Jesus? Which ones? How does that strengthen or weaken your relationship with Jesus (for example, do they draw you near, or cause you to step back from intimacy)?

  - o Describe in detail what the Holy Spirit is like and your relationship with him. The Bible refers to the Holy Spirit as our counselor and comforter. These qualities remind many people of their mom. Picture in your mind your mom. Are you tempted to apply characteristics of Mom to the Holy Spirit? If so, which ones? How does that strengthen or weaken your relationship with the Holy Spirit (for example, do they draw you near, or cause you to step back from intimacy)?

Why is it important to explore our tendency to relate and compare? The only way we have to reconcile what it means to have a relationship with God, is to think about what it means to have a relationship with others. The problem is people are not perfect. We hurt each other, especially those in our own family that we love most. We often carry unresolved feelings of hurt, disappointment, anger, frustration and even unforgiveness. Unresolved feelings create triggers which can work their way into our relationship with the Godhead. For example, the woman who never felt loved by her father will find it difficult to feel loved by Father God. The man betrayed by his friend may find it difficult to trust in Jesus as a friend. The woman whose mother walked out or abandoned her may feel unsafe when talking about the Holy Spirit. The reality is our hearts carry the wounds of the past into our relationship with God.

When you notice *heart dis-ease* stop and ask God to show you the root cause. Remember things come up so that he can clean them up! He wants to set us free. Perhaps he will show us that we need to forgive an offense or let go of a past disappointment. Do the work so that you may experience greater intimacy. Give yourself to the process of allowing God to search and show you what is in your heart.

What other influences have helped shaped your view of God (culture, parents, friends)?

Consider the answers you gave. How many are based on what you heard about each member of the trinity versus what you have personally experienced?

Daily Exercise: Practicing Rest

Do what refreshes you daily while practicing his presence.

Step One – Do What You Enjoy!

Remember to incorporate REST while doing what you enjoy.

R = Relax

E = Enter in

S = Steep

T = Talk with

This Works For Me!

My father was a wonderful man. There was never a doubt in my mind how much he loved me. Because he always made me feel special, it was easy to compare God to my daddy. But this exercise reminded me that God is NOT like my wonderful father. He is more. I'm still trying to wrap my arms around what this means in my life. Every day I tell myself as wonderful as my daddy was, God is all that and more. God loves me completely. God accepts me as I am. God is for me. I also now have compassion for others who have a different experience with their earthly fathers. I tell them to repeat the same truths and not to compare their earthly dads to Father God. —Julie K.

Step Two – Be Aware!

Note what you are feeling or sensing.

- Are you comfortable? Are you restless?
- If so, ask why.
- Write down what comes to your mind.

*Remember the goal is to be set free from anything
that hinders deeper intimacy with God.*

WEEKLY EXERCISE: PRACTICING REST

Do what refreshes you weekly while practicing God's presence.

STEP ONE — DO WHAT YOU LOVE TO DO TO FEEL REFRESHED.

Remember to incorporate REST while doing what you enjoy.

R = Relax

E = Enter in

S = Steep

T = Talk with

STEP TWO — RECORD WHAT YOU LEARNED

Make sure you record what you learned, felt, or heard in your *Strength Training Journal*.

Do you feel rested?

Finally, don't feel guilty if you can't do this daily or practice the once a week rest. But be AWARE. What obstacles came up? What is your plan to overcome the distractions next week? Make sure to write your plan down in your journal.

My Strength Training Journal

Keep track of what you learned this week. Take notes so you can share PRACTICAL *Strength Training* tips with your group.

What I learned about myself this week:

What I learned about God this week:

What I learned about *Strength Training* this week:

*Give yourself
to the process of
allowing God to
search and show you
what is in your heart.*

LEVEL 4: IDENTIFYING HEART DIS-EASE, PART 2

FOCUS

Strength is the result of being able to REST in the presence of the Lord. Jesus longs to spend time with you. He beckons you to *come to* and *learn of him* as you exchange weariness and heavy burdens for the peace found in his presence. His desire is for you know him through experience, not just intellect. He invites you to intimacy.

People in general have misconceptions about who God is (his character), how he sees you, and how he relates to you. Instead of drawing near and finding the comfort, rest, refreshment, acceptance and love that is available in relationship with him, many pull back. They experience *heart dis-ease* when they try to practice his presence. Instead of peace, they experience restlessness, making it difficult to develop the personal intimate relationship he offers.

In order to prevent *heart dis-ease* we can check our hearts by practicing awareness of our feelings and attitudes. We can ask ourselves, what do I believe to be true about God? Have I been taught the truth about the character of God the Father, Holy Spirit, and Jesus? Have I been influenced by culture's opinion about him? Do I practice outcome management with God; meaning, "Do I expect God to do what I ask for?" Is my relationship with him being affected by *relationship replay*, which is associating the character of God with the character of someone I had, or do have, a relationship with?

It is important to capture our thoughts and focus on what is true of God. If we don't believe the truth about him we can't experience a true intimate relationship. He is perfect and the relationship he offers us is perfect because he relates to us perfectly.

- He is the perfect father.
- He is the perfect friend.
- He is the perfect sibling.
- He is the perfect bridegroom.
- He is the perfect comforter.
- He is the perfect counselor.

Experiencing the presence of God helps us believe in the perfection of God. The more time we spend with him, the more we come to understand how he is the perfect father, the perfect friend, the perfect counselor, etc. As our experiential knowledge and understanding of him grows we find it easier to hear his voice and REST in his presence.

How consistent were you last week with your *Strength Training* and REST exercises?

Are you becoming more successful connecting with God? Are you finding it easier to be aware of his presence? Explain.

What obstacles or challenges are coming up?

Have you been able to discern his voice? (Remember, God speaks to each of us differently. Sometimes we hear a voice in our mind, we see an image, have an impression, a feeling, or we will be reminded of a Bible verse.) If our impressions align with God's Word, his character, and his will revealed in his Word, we can trust what we see and hear as God speaking to us. Remember, he will never tell you something that contradicts his Word.

Have you learned anything new about God?

Have you learned anything new about yourself?

Did you discover any *heart dis-ease* or restlessness as you practiced his presence?

SEEING MYSELF AS GOD SEES ME

There is another factor that contributes to *heart dis-ease* in his presence…our *sense of self*. *Sense of self* is our feelings about our own identity and uniqueness. Sense of self answers the question, "Who am I?" Our sense of self is developed over time and is based on an accumulation of beliefs we have about ourselves. A negative sense of self can prevent a person from being comfortable in the presence of God AND others. The strongest indicator of sense of self is self-talk. What we say about ourselves, and to ourselves, reveals what we believe to be true about who we are.

What are the top things you frequently say to yourself?

When I make a mistake, I say: _____

When I look in the mirror, I say: _____

When someone is unhappy with me, I say: _____

When I think about my past, I say: _____

Look closely at your self-talk above. How does it sound: mean, critical, abusive, unkind, or something else? _____

What does your self-talk teach you about how you view yourself?

EXPLORE

Critical self-talk is an indication I am not seeing myself through God's eyes but through man's. *Heart dis-ease* happens when the "I-factor" gets in the way. The I-factor is how I see myself—both good and bad—and I believe God sees me the same way. Instead of drawing near to him we back away in fear, afraid he rejects us. This is not a new problem; we can trace this reaction back to the fall of man.

Highlight or underline any words or phrases that stand out to you in the following passage.

> *The serpent was the shrewdest of all the wild animals the LORD God had made.*
> *One day he asked the woman, "Did God really say you must not eat the fruit from*
> *any of the trees in the garden? Of course we may eat fruit from the trees*
> *in the garden," the woman replied. "It's only the fruit from the tree in the middle of*
> *the garden that we are not allowed to eat. God said, 'You must not eat it or even*
> *touch it; if you do, you will die.' " "You won't die!" the serpent replied to the woman.*
> *"God knows that your eyes will be opened as soon as you eat it, and you will*
> *be like God, knowing both good and evil." The woman was convinced. She saw that*

the tree was beautiful and its fruit looked delicious, and she wanted the wisdom it would give her. So she took some of the fruit and ate it. Then she gave some to her husband, who was with her, and he ate it, too. At that moment their eyes were opened, and they suddenly felt shame at their nakedness. So they sewed fig leaves together to cover themselves. When the cool evening breezes were blowing, the man and his wife heard the LORD God walking about in the garden. So they hid from the LORD God among the trees. Then the LORD God called to the man, "Where are you?" He replied, "I heard you walking in the garden, so I hid. I was afraid because I was naked." "Who told you that you were naked?" the LORD God asked. "Have you eaten from the tree whose fruit I commanded you not to eat?" The man replied, "It was the woman you gave me who gave me the fruit, and I ate it." Then the LORD God asked the woman, "What have you done?" "The serpent deceived me," she replied. "That's why I ate it."

Genesis 3:1–13 (NLT)

Immediately upon eating the fruit of the *tree of the knowledge of good and evil,* Adam and Eve's eyes were opened and they realized their nakedness and felt shame. They covered their nakedness from each other and hid from God. What changed?

1. For the first time in their lives they were suddenly self-aware. Prior to the fall, Adam and Eve were perfectly united with God and each other. They were not focused on themselves but rather wholly devoted to the Lord, caring for creation and each other. Their love was perfect, not yet polluted by pride and self-centeredness.

2. For the first time they no longer saw themselves through God's eyes, but through the perspective of fallen man. Before they ate, they knew they were good and created in God's image, because God said so. Covering themselves and hiding from God, after they ate, revealed their self-condemnation and shame. They no longer believed they were good, they believed they were bad. Shame is a paralyzing emotion that defines a person and warps their sense of self. It is important to understand that shame is very different from guilt. Guilt says, "I did something bad or wrong." Shame says, "Because I did something bad I am bad."

The issue is not whether Adam and Eve were bad. The issue is what they now believed to be true about themselves because they *did something* bad. Did God love Adam and Eve any less? Did God stop calling Adam and Eve good because of their sin? Do you believe consequences for sinful actions equal God's rejection?

Highlight or underline any words or phrases that stand out to you in the following passage.

> *Then the LORD God said to the serpent, "Because you have done this, you are*
> *cursed more than all animals, domestic and wild. You will crawl on your belly,*
> *groveling in the dust as long as you live. And I will cause hostility between you and*
> *the woman, and between your offspring and her offspring. He will strike your*
> *head, and you will strike his heel." Then he said to the woman, "I will sharpen*
> *the pain of your pregnancy, and in pain you will give birth. And you will desire to*
> *control your husband, but he will rule over you." And to the man he said, "Since you*
> *listened to your wife and ate from the tree whose fruit I commanded you not to eat,*
> *the ground is cursed because of you. All your life you will struggle to scratch a living*
> *from it. It will grow thorns and thistles for you, though you will eat of its*
> *grains. By the sweat of your brow will you have food to eat until you return to the*
> *ground from which you were made. For you were made from dust, and to dust you*
> *will return." Then the man—Adam—named his wife Eve, because she would be the*
> *mother of all who live. And the LORD God made clothing from animal skins for*
> *Adam and his wife. Then the LORD God said, "Look, the human beings*
> *have become like us, knowing both good and evil. What if they reach out, take*
> *fruit from the tree of life, and eat it? Then they will live forever!" So the LORD*
> *God banished them from the Garden of Eden, and he sent Adam out to cultivate*
> *the ground from which he had been made. After sending them out, the LORD God*
> *stationed mighty cherubim to the east of the Garden of Eden.*
> *And he placed a flaming sword that flashed back and forth to*
> *guard the way to the tree of life.*
>
> Genesis 3:14–24 (NLT)

God loved Adam and Eve. When they disobeyed him he didn't stop being their Father, loving them, or having a relationship with them. He did however, discipline them...after all, that is what a loving father does.

> *It's the child he loves that he disciplines;*
> *the child he embraces, he also corrects.*
>
> Hebrews 12:6 (The Message)

What was loving about the consequences for their actions? Now fallen due to disobedience, what would have happened had Adam and Eve eaten from the *Tree of Life*? They would have lived forever as fallen, and therefore separated from God. In love, God protected them, not punished them. The purpose of discipline is to correct behavior that is harmful. Discipline is good for us. It reminds us of the boundaries God has put in place and helps us to make better decisions the next time. In fact, discipline should remind us that we are loved, forgiven and valued. Discipline redirects our focus from self to God.

Many people misunderstand God's actions. They believe sending Adam and Eve from the Garden of Eden was a form of rejection. Once away from the perfect environment of the Garden, they were faced with a choice. They could choose to depend on God and draw strength from an intimate relationship with him. Or, in their self-awareness, live independent of God.

Imagine the relational devastation left in the wake of the fall. Eve gave Adam the fruit from the tree. Adam blamed Eve for his choice to eat the fruit. Adam had to work the ground to provide food. Eve would experience pain in childbirth. She longed to control her husband but he ruled over her. No longer were they equals and a power struggle ensued. Imagine their conversations and self-talk. Once they had children, one brother killed the other. Adam and Eve's thoughts and self-condemnation may have colored their conversations and occupied their thoughts with phrases like:

- I'm a failure.
- You destroyed our life!
- I messed up a good thing.
- God must hate me.
- This is your fault.
- I'm worthless.
- I never should have listened to the serpent.
- I'm so stupid.

It is easy to understand how their experiences could create a negative sense of self and *heart dis-ease* in God's presence. No longer could they easily define themselves as "good." They would have to ask, seek, and pray to hear the still small voice of the Lord whispering his love, acceptance and guidance.

Can you relate? Have you allowed your sense of self to be defined by your mistakes?

Have you allowed the opinion of others to affect what you believe to be true about yourself? Explain.

The truth is, God's perspective of who we are is based in his love for us. In relationship, he teaches us to see ourselves through his eyes. Over time the beliefs we have about our identity are refined as he lovingly reveals his heart for us.

When we experience *heart dis-ease* in God's presence, we must check to see if our sense of self is causing us to cower and hide from him. Do you believe lies about your identity? Truthfully, it is very common to have an inaccurate sense of self. When we are restless in his presence we can perform a heart check by asking God and ourselves the following questions.

Do I Believe I Am Loved?

Do you believe God loves you personally and unconditionally? Why do you believe it? If you struggle to believe he loves you, what experiences in your life have created this doubt?

While we know God loves us, most of us struggle to receive God's love. Human beings love one another conditionally. Broken relationships are common in our experience. Love becomes performance driven. We easily shift into people pleaser mode, doing all we can, to keep the relationship alive. After all, no one wants to feel the sting of rejection. No matter what your human experience is, God doesn't reject you. You don't have to please him in order to earn his love because it's not based on performance. He simply loves you. Nothing can keep you from his love but your beliefs. Perhaps that's why Paul said:

*I pray that from his glorious, unlimited resources he will empower you with inner
strength through his Spirit. Then Christ will make his home in your hearts as you
trust in him. Your roots will grow down into God's love and keep you strong.
And may you have the power to understand, as all God's people should, how wide,
how long, how high, and how deep his love is. May you experience the love of
Christ, though it is too great to understand fully. Then you will be made complete
with all the fullness of life and power that comes from God.*

Ephesians 3:16–19 (NLT)

When you are tempted to believe you are not loved, *stop*! Instead say aloud:

❤ I AM Says, I am loved. Therefore, I choose to believe him over how I feel, and I will
not give in to the temptation to try earn his love.

Do I Believe I Am Good Enough?

Do you judge yourself and your actions? What things do you say to yourself?

Do you beat yourself up for doing the same old things over and over again? If so, do your
actions cause you to question how God could ever love you or long to have a relationship
with you? Explain?

Feeling *not good enough* comes from self-judgment. Most of the time we evaluate
everything—our behavior, personality, looks, intelligence, etc.—based on comparison. Our
sense of self is developed, in large part, by comparing ourselves with others. We also tend to
have high expectations of ourselves which are often absent of grace. When we fall short of
our own standards and expectations, our nature is to beat ourselves up verbally and believe
the lie *we'll never learn, we'll never change*. We believe, in error, that being good enough is
dependent entirely on our ability to act "good enough" and do enough of the "right things."
In truth we are good enough not because of who we are, or what we do, but because of *whose*
we are. As followers of Jesus we are on a journey toward perfection, but it is a journey, not a
destination. We are transformed in our day to day, moment by moment, intimate walk with

Jesus. Receive the grace he gives you. He makes you good enough. Remember, your old self is dead and Christ is living *his* life through you!

> *My old self has been crucified with Christ. It is no longer I who live,*
> *but Christ lives in me. So I live in this earthly body by trusting in*
> *the Son of God, who loved me and gave himself for me.*
>
> Galatians 2:20 (NLT)

When you are tempted to believe you are not good enough, stop! Instead say aloud:

♥ I AM Says, I am good enough because Christ lives in me! I believe I am living this life by trusting in God who loved me and gave himself for me, and that is why I'm good enough!

Do I Feel Shame?

Shame can be heard in our self-talk and felt in our body. You may experience a sick or sinking feeling in your stomach or have difficultly looking into someone's eyes. When you think back over your mistakes, which ones have created that sense or feeling of shame?

Feeling not good enough, or unworthy, is caused by a shame based identity. As we learned earlier, shame is different than guilt. When our actions are wrong or sinful, guilt fills our hearts and our conscience is affected. Guilt makes us aware of our sinful actions and attitudes and is a helpful aide to correct our behavior. Shame amplifies guilt. Instead of our actions being sinful and therefore correctable, shame causes a person to believe they *are* a bad person. The mistakes they made become that person's identity: the person who lied is always a liar, the promiscuous girl is always the slut, etc. In our minds we become our sin. Shame then defines who we are and we spend our lives trying to cover ourselves and hide from God. We believe the lie that we are beyond his ability to help us. *After all, why would God want to help me—I'm just a* _____. Shame is a powerful mindset because it keeps us from experiencing God's grace, forgiveness and transformation. Shame is a trap that robs the believer of their true identity in Jesus. We do not have to accept shame. The Bible teaches:

Those who look to him are radiant; their faces are never covered with shame.

Psalm 34:5 (NIV)

Overcoming shame is as simple as looking to Jesus. A big part of practicing REST in your *Strength Training* time is talking with the Lord about the things you've done that cause you to feel shame. He wants you to see yourself as he does, his priceless treasure. He wants you to know he died to set you free from your mistakes and wrong beliefs about who you are. He has forgiven you and he wants you to forgive yourself. That is grace in action! He wants you to know the same power that resurrected him from the grave can resurrect you from the paralyzing power of shame. You can experience the abundant, transformed life. The more we practice his presence and listen to his voice, the more we are able to receive the truth about who we are…a new creation.

Therefore if any person is [ingrafted] in Christ (the Messiah) he is a new creation (a new creature altogether); the old [previous moral and spiritual condition] has passed away. Behold, the fresh and new has come!

2 Corinthians 5:17 (AMP)

When you are tempted to allow shame to dominate your life and affect your identity, or if you want to climb out of the pit of shame, simply say—STOP!

- ♥ I AM says if anyone is in me (Christ), he is a new creation; the old has gone, the new has come! (2 Corinthians 5:17 NIV)

THE CURE FOR HEART DIS-EASE

The cure for *heart dis-ease* is regular daily doses of truth and experiencing intimacy with the great I AM…I AM is God's name. Both Father God and Jesus called themselves I AM (see Exodus 3:14 and John 8:58). It is his personal name. It is amazing to know we enjoy intimacy with I AM!

The word of God is living and active. It is our defense against *heart dis-ease* caused by incorrect mindsets. God's Word, his truth, trumps the lies that keep us trapped in the belief that we need to hide from God. When we speak God's Word out loud affirming who we are in Jesus we rob the enemy of his power to accuse us and we destroy shame once and for all. As believers we are instructed to …*demolish arguments and every pretension that sets itself* up against the knowledge of God, and we take captive every thought to make it obedient to Christ (2 Corinthians 10:5 NIV).

Every thought that creates a disturbance in our heart or mind, or tempts us to hide from God, must be captured and compared with the truth of Scripture. Test your thoughts about who God is, how he relates to us, and how he sees us, with the Word! This practice teaches you to recognize deception and overcome it with the truth. God's Word is our powerful weapon against the lies that cause *heart dis-ease.*

> *For though we live in the world, we do not wage war as the world does.*
> *The weapons we fight with are not the weapons of the world. On the contrary,*
> *they have divine power to demolish strongholds.*
>
> 2 Corinthians 10:3–4 (NIV)

God's weapons are available for God's children to use. Have you placed your faith in Jesus and what he did for you on the cross? Until we answer this question affirmatively, practicing the presence of God, *Strength Training* and REST, as well as overcoming incorrect mindsets, will be impossible. God is real and he is available to you personally. He desires an intimate relationship with you. But, it is a choice that must be intentionally made by each of us.

How to Start a Relationship With Jesus

You have been told over and over throughout this study that God loves you. He created you in his image and likeness and his desire is for you to know him. People often talk about the joy of having a "personal relationship" with God. A relationship with Jesus begins when we embrace his life, death, and resurrection as his personal gift to free us from our sin. It involves not just believing, but intentionally following him and living obedient to his Word to the best of our understanding.

What is sin? The Bible says that all wrongdoing is sin. Sin is anything we do that is contrary to how the Bible says we should live. James 4:17 says, *remember, it is sin to know what you ought to do and then not do it* (NLT). Sin isn't just our wrong actions, it includes our wrong attitudes as well. The truth is, we all sin. The Bible, which is God's written words to us, says that we all fall short—we all miss the mark—all of us. Because God is holy, he can't be near sin. So our mistakes separate us from God. More than that, there is a high price that must be paid for sin. Romans 6:23 says, *For the wages of sin is death* (NIV). But here is the Good News: God provided a way to wipe away our mistakes and reunite us with him. He sent his Son,

Jesus Christ. Jesus came to earth, lived a perfect life, and died on a cross to pay the price for our mistakes. He rose from the dead after three days, forever defeating the power of sin and death in our lives.

So what must I do to begin a relationship with God?

1. Admit. Admit that you make mistakes and sin.

2. Change the way you think—or repent. To repent simply means to think differently. We repent by telling God we are sorry for our mistakes, turning away from our sins and committing to following God's way.

3. Believe that Jesus Christ came to earth to pay the penalty for your sin.

4. Receive Jesus into your life. Romans 10:9–10 says:

> *If you confess with your mouth that Jesus is Lord and believe in your*
> *heart that God raised him from the dead, you will be saved. For it is by*
> *believing in your heart that you are made right with God, and it is by confessing*
> *with your mouth that you are saved* (NLT).

Say to Jesus, "I admit I need you. I believe you died on the cross as payment for my sin—thank you! I believe your resurrection defeated death once and for all. I believe you love me. I choose to follow you—to come to you—and begin an intimate relationship with you. Help me follow you. Amen"

A relationship with God is more than life insurance. It's an adventure. God is present in your life. Jesus is your friend. The Holy Spirit lives in you counseling, guiding, and empowering you. You are a member of the Kingdom of God and it is at hand! You are part of God's plan for this world and that is exciting! Cultivating intimacy with him strengthens you! This is why we are teaching you to Strength Train!

What Comes Next?

If you just prayed this prayer, share this exciting news with your small group leader or another believing friend right away. They can help guide you as you learn to walk with the Lord. Remember, the prayer is not what saves you, *it is believing in Jesus that saves you*. Believing is an everyday process of following Jesus, practicing his presence, talking with him, and applying his Word to your life.

May you grow every day in the experiential knowledge and love of the Lord.

Wrapping It Up

Heart dis-ease is a condition rooted in fear caused by a misconception about who God is, how God sees you and how he relates to you. It prevents a person from drawing near and being able to experience the love, comfort, rest, refreshment, acceptance and peace that comes from intimacy with him. When we have an inaccurate picture of who God is and how he relates to us we are unable to come to him without apprehension and dis-ease. One of the most telling signs of *heart dis-ease* is *restlessness*.

We must continually be aware of our thoughts and attitudes toward God and how we feel about spending time in his presence. To continuing growing in intimacy we must practice the cure for *heart dis-ease*.

- Daily doses of the truth found in God's Word.

- Complete honesty with ourselves and God about how we feel and what we think.

- A willing spirit to forgive ourselves, God, and others.

God's Heart for You

You are my Beautiful Child. I love you with an everlasting love. There is never a moment that you are not loved by me. There is never a time when you are not precious to me. I will always adore you. I created you with intricate detail; you are beautiful in my sight.

When your mind is cluttered with fears, doubts, concerns and worry I am standing with you through every moment. I sing over you because I delight in you.

Nothing you have done surprises me or causes me to love you any less. I love you with an everlasting love. You are mine and I delight to meet all your needs, especially your need for affirmation. Come to me when you are weary and burdened by the negative self-talk and expectations you have of yourself, and I will give you rest and soothe your soul. I desire for you to realize you are the apple of my eye.

You are my treasured possession. You are not a disappointment. You are my child. I take joy in watching you be you. I love you.

~~~~~~~~~~

Everlasting love; Jeremiah 31:3; Psalm 139. I created you...; Psalm 139:13–14. God's treasured possession; Ephesians 1:13–15. Sing over you; Zephaniah 3:17. I am with you always; Matthew 28:20. Come to me… and I will give you rest; Matthew 11:28. Apple of his eye...; Deuteronomy 32:9–1. Nothing you have done surprises me; Psalm 139:16.

SHARE

1. Review the lesson and discuss the questions that are interesting to your group.

2. Do you or anyone in your group struggle with negative self-talk and its damaging effects? If so take a moment to pray for that habit to be defeated.

3. A few of you share your experience with your attempts to spend time with the Lord.

4. If you feel comfortable, share how you felt as you left your time with God. Were you able to carry your connection with him into the rest of your day or for a little while? Remember, you may be starting a new chapter of your walk with the Lord and it will be a growing process.

5. Training with friends is always more fun than training alone. If you haven't joined a group of friends to encourage your training yet, be sure to do that before you leave the group today. For this study we recommend you connect with one or two others. Commit to encouraging one another over the remainder of this study. Practice 1 Thessalonians 5:11 and check-in with each other at least twice a week for support.

Therefore encourage (admonish, exhort) one another and edify
(strengthen and build up) one another, just as you are doing.
1 Thessalonians 5:11 (AMP)

STRENGTH TRAINING

GETTING STARTED:

This week we continued to identify the causes of *heart dis-ease*. For your *Strength Training* exercise, practice combining the presence of God with the daily REST Exercise that refreshes you. Be aware of your thoughts and feelings. Remember, we want to identify and stamp out *heart dis-ease* as it impacts our ability to be completely at ease with the Lord. If you discover that you are experiencing a feeling of restlessness, anxiety, fear, or shame STOP and SEARCH for the root cause.

Heart Check:

The questions below will help you discover what has shaped your view of God and how he relates to you. Answer thoughtfully. Ask the Lord to show you any misconceptions that could lead to *heart dis-ease* in his presence.

Begin with a HEART CHECK

- Have I made an effort to sit alone with God daily or at least three times a week?
- Am I struggling? Do I know why?
- What, if any, obstacles am I encountering?
- How can I overcome these?
- Am I truly willing to connect with God at an intimate level? If not, why?
- If my time with God is rewarding, who have I shared my thoughts with?
- What has my time with God, or the lack of it, revealed to me personally?

Daily Exercise: Practicing Rest

Do what refreshes you daily while practicing his presence.

Step One — Do What You Enjoy!

Remember to incorporate REST while doing what you enjoy

R = Relax

E = Enter in

S = Steep

T = Talk with

Spend time reflecting on what you have believed to be true about who God is, who you are in his sight, and how he relates to you.

This Works For Me!

When I experience *heart dis-ease* in how I see myself, I find Bible verses that encourage me. I like to write them on 3 x 5 cards or on my bathroom mirror. Then when I am feeling overwhelmed with all that I am "not," I read them over and over. It helps me to focus on what is true. This is how I take my thoughts captive. —Jerry

---

STEP TWO – BE AWARE!

Note what you are feeling or sensing.

- Are you comfortable? Are you restless? If so, ask why.
- Write down what comes to your mind.

Remember, the goal is to be set free from anything
that hinders deeper intimacy with God.

WEEKLY EXERCISE: PRACTICING REST

Do what refreshes you weekly while practicing God's presence.

Make sure you record what you learned, felt, or heard in your *Strength Training Journal*.

- Do you feel rested? Or are you feeling dis-ease?
- Use the *Curing Heart Dis-ease* worksheet at the end of this lesson to record any lies you have believed in these areas and how they made you feel. Lies are beliefs we have that are opposite of what God's Word says is true. We've learned they come from what we are taught when we are young, what we have learned through experience, relationship replay, and our beliefs about ourselves based on comparison and our mistakes.

- Using the *Treasure Trove* at the end of this lesson, and *Father's Love Letter* from last week, record what God says is true. Record how embracing the truth sets you free from *heart dis-ease* as you practice his presence.
- Finally, talk with God about what you are learning.

My Strength Training Journal

Keep track of what you learned this week. Take notes so you can share PRACTICAL *Strength Training* tips with your group.

What I learned about myself this week:

What I learned about God this week:

What I learned about *Strength Training* this week:

Curing *HEART DIS-EASE*
And you will know the truth and the truth will set you free. John 8:32

Lies I Believed...	How the lies affected my thoughts, emotions, actions, and attitude:	What God's Word says about the lie:	How embracing his truth sets me free:
About God:			
About Myself:			
About how God relates to me:			

THE TREASURE TROVE

I AM SAYS, "YOU ARE BLESSED TO BELIEVE."	LUKE 1:45
I AM SAYS, "YOU ARE SIGNIFICANT."	PROVERBS 16:4
I AM SAYS, "YOU ARE NOT YOUR OWN."	1 CORINTHIANS 7:23
I AM SAYS, "YOU ARE A CHILD OF GOD."	JOHN 1:12–13
I AM SAYS, "YOU ARE FREE FROM FEAR."	2 TIMOTHY 1:7
I AM SAYS, "YOU ARE MADE BY HIM."	PSALM 119:73
I AM SAYS, "YOU ARE BEAUTIFUL."	SONG OF SONGS 1:15
I AM SAYS, "YOU ARE RADIANT."	PSALM 34:5
I AM SAYS, "YOU ARE HEARD."	JEREMIAH 29:12
I AM SAYS, "YOU ARE KNOWN."	1 CORINTHIANS 8:3
I AM SAYS, "YOU ARE CAPABLE."	PHILIPPIANS 4:13
I AM SAYS, "YOU ARE CONFIDENT."	PROVERBS 3:26
I AM SAYS, "YOU ARE ACCEPTED."	EPHESIANS 1:6
I AM SAYS, "YOU ARE NOT SHAKEN."	PSALM 40:1–2
I AM SAYS, "YOU ARE A SAINT."	PSALM 30:4
I AM SAYS, "YOU ARE DELIGHTED IN."	ISAIAH 62:5
I AM SAYS, "YOU ARE PROTECTED."	PSALM 32:7
I AM SAYS, "YOU ARE UNIQUE."	SONG OF SONGS 6:9
I AM SAYS, "YOU ARE FREE."	JOHN 8:36
I AM SAYS, "YOU ARE CARED FOR."	PSALM 34:18
I AM SAYS, "YOU ARE GOOD."	GENESIS 1:31
I AM SAYS, "YOU ARE A NEW CREATION."	2 CORINTHIANS 5:17
I AM SAYS, "YOU ARE FORGIVEN."	ISAIAH 1:18
I AM SAYS, "YOU ARE A FINISHED WORK IN PROGRESS."	PHILIPPIANS 1:6
I AM SAYS, "YOU ARE MORE THAN A CONQUEROR."	ROMANS 8:35, 37
I AM SAYS, "YOU ARE TREASURED."	DEUTERONOMY 7:6
I AM SAYS, "YOU ARE SECURE."	DEUTERONOMY 33:12
I AM SAYS, "YOU ARE A WARRIOR."	GENESIS 2:18
I AM SAYS, "YOU ARE GIFTED."	ROMANS 12:6A
I AM SAYS, "YOU ARE ROYALTY."	ROMANS 8:15–17A
I AM SAYS, "YOU ARE LOVED."	JOHN 3:16–17

You will be able to
REST comfortably
in the completely loving
and trustworthy arms
of the one who loves you
perfectly.

LEVEL 5: TRAINING TO REIGN

FOCUS

We've learned that *heart dis-ease* is a condition rooted in fear caused by a misconception about who God is, how God sees you, and how he relates to you. It prevents a person from drawing near and being able to experience the love, comfort, rest, refreshment, acceptance and peace that comes from intimacy with him. When we have an inaccurate picture of who God is, and how he relates to us, we are unable to come to him without apprehension and dis-ease. One of the most telling signs of *heart dis-ease* is *restlessness*.

We must continually be aware of our thoughts and attitudes toward God and how we feel about spending time in his presence. We also must be mindful of our self-talk as it reveals what we believe to be true about our own identity. Negative self-talk reveals that we see ourselves through the world's perspective instead of God's. In order to experience greater intimacy with Jesus, we learned the importance of being aware of what we believe to be true about God and how he sees us.

Heart Dis-ease RX

Heart dis-ease can be cured through:

- Daily doses of the Truth
- Honesty with self and with God regarding my feelings
- A willing spirit to forgive self, others, and God

There are three factors that indicate we are becoming free from heart dis-ease: 1) an increased longing to be in his presence, 2) feeling comforted or at peace when we are with him, and 3) a willingness to allow him to deal with our heart and refine our character.

How consistent were you last week with your *Strength Training* and REST exercises?

Are you becoming more successful connecting with God? Describe what is different or new.

Are you finding it easier to be aware of his presence throughout your day? Explain.

What obstacles or challenges are you experiencing? How are you handling them?

EXPLORE

TRAINING TO REIGN

As we grow in intimacy with God it becomes easier to trust him. Trust is essential. When beginning his ministry Jesus called a handful of men to be his disciples. As their relationship deepened, Jesus began to train them to reign.

In a relationship built on trust, he began to refine their character by teaching and modeling how they should live. His goal was not only to save them (and all of us) from sin, but to transform both attitude and actions. As they followed him, gently (and sometimes forcefully) Jesus would expose areas of thinking and behavior that needed transformation. He challenged them to grow in the way they reacted and interacted. There were tests, trials and even temptations that strengthened them in areas where they were weak. He taught them to appreciate and even see beauty in brokenness. He commanded them to love one another because love proved, to the watching world, they were his disciples. He was training them to reign by training them to be more than conquerors, but overcomers.

You, too, are being trained to reign. Every day God is at work transforming you from the inside out. This is why, as we practice the presence of God, we must continue to submit to the coaching and training of the Holy Spirit in our lives as he: EXPOSES AREAS OF OUR HEARTS THAT NEED REFINEMENT OR REMOVAL.

We all have room for character improvement. It is the Holy Spirit within us that powers character renewal. The more time we spend in his presence the stronger we become in our ability to naturally walk in his Spirit. Paul says, as we walk with the Lord we grow in the fruit of his Spirit.

> *But I say, walk and live [habitually] in the [Holy] Spirit [responsive to and controlled and guided by the Spirit]; then you will certainly not gratify the cravings and desires of the flesh (of human nature without God).*
>
> Galatians 5:16 (AMP)

We know we are growing in him as his characteristics become visible in our attitudes and actions.

♥ Training to reign is growing up in Jesus.

GUIDES US TO RECOGNIZE AND EMBRACE OUR BROKENNESS.

> *...for you are a chosen people. You are royal priests, a holy nation, God's very own possession. As a result, you can show others the goodness of God, for he called you out of the darkness into his wonderful light.*
>
> 1 Peter 2:9 (NLT)

As a holy priesthood, we have been given the opportunity to embrace the broken places in our hearts and lives and use them to show the greatness of God. We are invited to partner with the Lord and his work of freeing the captives. Sharing our own journey, comforting others with the comfort he has given us, and speaking the truth in love, are all responsibilities of the royal priests. We shine the light of his redemptive work in the world. His spirit will direct and guide you in what to share and when.

💜 Training to reign is embracing the beautiful role of a royal priest.

ENCOURAGES US TO LOVE AS EVIDENCE THAT WE BELONG TO HIM

Your love for one another will prove to the world that you are my disciples.
John 13:35 (NLT)

As we practice his presence and walk by his Spirit we will find it easier to love others. Love is the evidence we belong to him. It is the hallmark of the transformed heart. As we walk with him, he will teach us to love by sharing, confronting, listening, walking with and having compassion for one another. His Spirit will move us to act on behalf of others, to come alongside the hurting and the broken, to stand in faith in battle, to pray, to carry a part of a load too heavy for the hurting to handle.

💜 Training to reign is learning to walk in love.

Training to reign is really about walking out our relationship with Jesus through the power and direction of the Holy Spirit. It is living our faith.

Training to reign is learning to walk as Jesus did; in faith not fear, ready and willing to act, interruptible, joyful, patient and peaceful.

Because God is more concerned with our character than our comfort, expect to experience 24-hour fitness and continuous teachable moments. Be aware he will *always* be at work in two primary areas:

1. Our faith, because …*without faith it is impossible to please Him…* Hebrews 11:6 (NASB)

2. Our character (which is the mental and moral qualities distinctive to an individual), because *we...are being transformed into his likeness with ever-increasing glory, which comes from the Lord, who is the Spirit* (2 Corinthians 3:18 NIV).

Faith and character have to be tested in order to be proven. We must learn to trust the Lord in the common day to day activities of life, and with the unforeseen and unexpected events that come out of nowhere. Tests and trials reveal where we are weak or lacking in faith or character. In the safety of a relationship built on trust, we can learn to embrace our problems and even see them as opportunities to experience more of his love and power.

> *We can rejoice, too, when we run into problems and trials, for we know that they help us develop endurance. And endurance develops strength of character, and character strengthens our confident hope of salvation. And this hope will not lead to disappointment. For we know how dearly God loves us, because he has given us the Holy Spirit to fill our hearts with his love.*
>
> Romans 5:3–5 (NLT)

The biggest obstacle to strengthening and growing our faith is fear. Over and over again Jesus told the disciples and people who came to him not to fear but believe: *...Jesus told the synagogue ruler, "Don't be afraid; just believe"* (Mark 5:36b NIV).

Why?

> *For God hath not given us the spirit of fear; but of power, and of love, and of a sound mind.*
>
> 2 Timothy 1:7 (KJV)

That is why training to reign involves giant slaying. As we face our fears we grow in strength. Over and over David, called a man after God's own heart, experienced many challenges and problems. Obviously, being in relationship with God doesn't mean problem free living. But, David saw each new test or problem as an opportunity for him to experience more of God's presence and power. David was a mighty man of God but he didn't start off that way. He had to strength train just like us in order to grow in faith. David's training included giant slaying.

BECOMING A GIANT SLAYER

Highlight or underline any words or phrases that are interesting to you in the passages below.

> *Now the Philistines gathered their armies for battle; and they were gathered at Socoh which belongs to Judah, and they camped between Socoh and Azekah, in Ephes-dammim. Saul and the men of Israel were gathered and camped in the valley of Elah, and drew up in battle array to encounter the Philistines. The Philistines stood on the mountain on one side while Israel stood on the mountain on the other side, with the valley between them. Then a champion came out from the armies of the Philistines named Goliath, from Gath, whose height was six cubits and a span. He had a bronze helmet on his head, and he was clothed with scale-armor which weighed five thousand shekels of bronze. He also had bronze greaves on his legs and a bronze javelin slung between his shoulders. The shaft of his spear was like a weaver's beam, and the head of his spear weighed six hundred shekels of iron; his shield-carrier also walked before him.*
>
> 1 Samuel 17:1–7 (NASB)

Goliath was a giant sized problem that came to Israel and invaded their territory. He was intimidating both in size and stature. He was daunting and fearsome to look at. He was also well protected. His armor made him look undefeatable and he even had a shield bearer. Training to reign often involves facing something that appears bigger and stronger than you are.

What is your Goliath? In your life are there any problems or circumstances that appear giant sized? Describe them. Due to the way it looks, do you feel overwhelmed when you think of having to face it? Why or why not.

He stood and shouted to the ranks of Israel and said to them, "Why do you come out to draw up in battle array? Am I not the Philistine and you servants of Saul? Choose a man for yourselves and let him come down to me. "If he is able to fight with me and kill me, then we will become your servants; but if I prevail against him and kill him, then you shall become our servants and serve us." Again the Philistine said, "I defy the ranks of Israel this day; give me a man that we may fight together." When Saul and all Israel heard these words of the Philistine, they were dismayed and greatly afraid. Now David was the son of the Ephrathite of Bethlehem in Judah, whose name was Jesse, and he had eight sons. And Jesse was old in the days of Saul, advanced in years among men. The three older sons of Jesse had gone after Saul to the battle. And the names of his three sons who went to the battle were Eliab the firstborn, and the second to him Abinadab, and the third Shammah. David was the youngest. Now the three oldest followed Saul, but David went back and forth from Saul to tend his father's flock at Bethlehem. The Philistine came forward morning and evening for forty days and took his stand.

1 Samuel 17:8–16 (NASB)

Not only do giant sized problems have a way of intimidating us, they also taunt us. They shout at us and cause us to feel dismayed and greatly afraid. To be dismayed is to feel anxious, perplexed (confused) or fearful. Fear is the very opposite of faith. Fear weakens and paralyzes us from taking action. Fear sends us into self-evaluation and causes us to ask, "Am I strong enough to overcome this problem?" Fear undermines faith causing us to forget what God can do.

When Goliath yelled at Israel to send a man out to fight him, he said:

- *Are you not the servants of Saul?*
- *Choose a man…*
- *Let him come down to me…*
- *If he beats me we will serve you, but if I kill him you will serve me…*
- *Give me a man that we may fight together…*

Goliath-sized problems tempt us to come down from the mountain and engage the enemy on his terms. We face problems, not in our strength, power or ability, but in God's. Goliath called Israel the servants of Saul, when in reality they were the Lord's servants. They were God's chosen people, not Saul's. As we face problems, we must remember whose we are. We must also remember that God is the one who fights every battle with us.

Israel forgot who they belonged to. Because they fell into fear, they felt ill equipped and unprepared to face Goliath. Goliath taunted them for forty days and forty nights. Each day they became more and more afraid and fled when they saw Goliath.

- Did they forget Israel's deliverance from Egypt?

- Did fear cause them to forget the Red Sea?

- Did fear cause them to forget forty years with God in the desert?

- Did they forget the battle of Jericho?

WARNING: Avoidance never leads to deliverance!

When we are strength training we cannot forget the victories of the past. Those memories should be the basis for our perspective as we fight the good fight of faith.

Are you experiencing fear or dismay as you face your problem or circumstance? What are you focusing on? The longer we avoid confronting the problem, the more intimating it becomes, and the more power it has over us. Record your thoughts here as a prayer.

When we avoid a problem we are intentionally giving it power. Ignoring or avoiding problems doesn't make them go away. Instead we are actually feeding our own fears. Fear keeps us from trusting that God is at work providing for our victory. Fear causes us to forget who we are and whose we are.

What are you avoiding? What have you allowed to have power over you? What, if anything, is stopping you from taking action?

NEVER GIVE UP YOUR STRATEGIC POSITION IN A FIGHT! STAY SEATED IN HEAVENLY REALMS. (Ephesians 2:6)

So David arose early in the morning and left the flock with a keeper and took the supplies and went as Jesse had commanded him. And he came to the circle of the camp while the army was going out in battle array shouting the war cry. Israel and the Philistines drew up in battle array, army against army. Then David left his baggage in the care of the baggage keeper, and ran to the battle line and entered in order to greet his brothers. As he was talking with them, behold, the champion, the Philistine from Gath named Goliath, was coming up from the army of the Philistines, and he spoke these same words; and David heard them. When all the men of Israel saw the man, they fled from him and were greatly afraid. The men of Israel said, "Have you seen this man who is coming up? Surely he is coming up to defy Israel. And it will be that the king will enrich the man who kills him with great riches and will give him his daughter and make his father's house free in Israel." Then David spoke to the men who were standing by him, saying, "What will be done for the man who kills this Philistine and takes away the reproach from Israel? For who is this uncircumcised Philistine, that he should taunt the armies of the living God?" The people answered him in accord with this word, saying, "Thus it will be done for the man who kills him."

1 Samuel 17:20–27 (NASB)

When we encounter problems our response, when rooted in faith, should be the same as David's.

1. First we must leave our baggage behind. Don't bring baggage to the battle! Instead, approach it as a new experience. The only thing we need to take with us is the reality of God's presence. Leave behind disappointments, expectations, and memories of past problems.

What baggage are you dragging into your current situation?

2. Approach the problem expectantly. David asked what would be done for the man who kills the Philistine and takes away the reproach from Israel. Translated to today's language, he asked, "What am I going to get for dealing with this problem?" When I partner with God and attack this problem or circumstance head on, how will I benefit? David expected something good to come from this problem. The truth is, God always trades up (Isaiah 61:1–3).

When you encounter a problem, are you David or are you Israel? Do you shake in fear, or declare in faith, "What will be done for me?" What do you expect?

Now Eliab his oldest brother heard when he spoke to the men; and Eliab's anger burned against David and he said, "Why have you come down? And with whom have you left those few sheep in the wilderness? I know your insolence and the wickedness of your heart; for you have come down in order to see the battle." But David said, "What have I done now? Was it not just a question?" Then he turned away from him to another and said the same thing; and the people answered the same thing as before.

1 Samuel 17:28–30 (NASB)

3. David was faced with a challenge to his identity. Instead of engaging his older brother Eliab when challenged and demeaned, David turned away. Recognize that not everyone will want you to defeat your problems. They will try to hinder you with their own baggage. Eliab ridiculed David and intended to tear down his confidence and undermine his character. Why? Why would a member of his own family be so hateful and critical of David's motives?

In 1 Samuel 16 we are told that Samuel traveled to David's family's house in order to anoint the next king of Israel. Upon entering the house Samuel immediately encountered Eliab.

> *When they entered, he looked at Eliab and thought, "Surely the LORD'S anointed is before Him." But the LORD said to Samuel, "Do not look at his appearance or at the height of his stature, because I have rejected him; for God sees not as man sees, for man looks at the outward appearance, but the LORD looks at the heart."*
>
> 1 Samuel 16:6–7 (NASB)

When facing our problems, big or small, we must remember that the Lord has been teaching us to overcome the *heart dis-ease* that tempts us to believe we are not who he says we are. David had to recognize he was more than just a shepherd, he was God's anointed. We too are God's anointed. No matter what someone else may call you, God is the one who defines who you are. Don't listen to voices that try to undermine your faith and create fear. Instead stand firm in what God says is true of you because it is necessary for you to gain victory over your problems.

When someone tries to undermine your faith, turn away. A friend of mine recently lost her dream home. She and her husband had worked for years to build the perfect house. Unfortunately, the down turn in the economy affected their business. She fought and stood in faith believing that God would provide a way for them to keep the house. She prayed for more work to come their way and she trusted that God had his best in mind for her. While fighting to keep her home she had to turn away from people who, because of their own fear, undermined her faith with their "words of encouragement." Phrases like "just sell it," or "let it go" were not helping, but hurting. When facing fear filled problems, be careful who you listen to. Do what God tells you to do until he tells you otherwise. If he says believe. Believe. If he says fight. Fight. If he says wait. Wait. Don't be influenced or moved by the baggage other people bring to your battle. Stay strong in his Spirit. Remember…

> *For God did not give us a spirit of timidity, but a spirit of power, of love and of self-discipline.*
>
> 2 Timothy 1:7 (NIV)

> *When the words which David spoke were heard, they told them to Saul, and he sent for him. David said to Saul, "Let no man's heart fail on account of him; your servant will go and fight with this Philistine." Then Saul said to David, "You are not able to go against this Philistine to fight with him; for you are but a youth while he has been a warrior from his youth." But David said to Saul, "Your servant was tending his father's sheep. When a lion or a bear came and took a lamb from the flock, I went out after him and attacked him, and rescued it from his mouth; and when he rose up against me, I seized him by his beard and struck him and killed him. "Your servant has killed both the lion and the bear; and this uncircumcised Philistine will be like one of them, since he has taunted the armies of the living God." And David said, "The LORD who delivered me from the paw of the lion and from the paw of the bear, He will deliver me from the hand of this Philistine." And Saul said to David, "Go, and may the LORD be with you." Then Saul clothed David with his garments and put a bronze helmet on his head, and he clothed him with armor. David girded his sword over his armor and tried to walk, for he had not tested them. So David said to Saul, "I cannot go with these, for I have not tested them." And David took them off.*

1 Samuel 17:31–39 (NASB)

4. After overcoming the question of his identity, David was faced with having to overcome the perception of others regarding his ability.

   - He was young and inexperienced – *you are not able - you are but a youth*
   - He was not properly equipped – *Saul clothed David*

Despite what Saul thought, David *was* able. David realized God had trained and prepared him for this day. He had been taught to be courageous by protecting the flock he cared for. He had killed, with his bare hands, both the lion and the bear. For David, battling Goliath was part of the process that God had already begun in him. His faith was in what God had already empowered him to do. He needed a certain amount of strength to face the lion, and ever more to face the bear, both of which God provided. His experience with God taught him that God would deliver him. When Saul tried to clothe David in his armor, David knew Saul's protection was not God's provision. David trusted in God alone. His covering was sufficient for David.

Are you as confident in God and his deliverance as David? Our confidence for facing today's Goliaths should come from recognizing the lion and bear moments of our past. If God equipped us for those experiences, why wouldn't he equip us for our present problem?

In addition, because David walked with God he knew God's will. Goliath was defying the armies of the living God. He and the Philistines had invaded the land of Judah, the land God had already promised to Israel. David was able because he knew what God wanted. He didn't need to pray about it, believe for it, or fast for an answer. He just needed to act. So many times victory is already ours, but we don't act. Training to reign includes knowing, recognizing, and acting upon the will of God.

WE KNOW THE WILL OF GOD BY KNOWING THE WORD OF GOD

> *Do not be conformed to this world (this age), [fashioned after and adapted to its external, superficial customs], but be transformed (changed) by the [entire] renewal of your mind [by its new ideals and its new attitude], so that you may prove [for yourselves] what is the good and acceptable and perfect will of God, even the thing which is good and acceptable and perfect [in His sight for you].*

Romans 12:2 (AMP)

Training to reign involves remembering what God has done and how he has worked in the past. We can draw strength from what God has taught us, and how he has equipped and empowered us. And David acted because he knew God's perfect will.

What lessons from your past give you *God confidence* in your present problems?

He took his stick in his hand and chose for himself five smooth stones from the brook, and put them in the shepherd's bag which he had, even in his pouch, and his sling was in his hand; and he approached the Philistine. Then the Philistine came on and approached David, with the shield-bearer in front of him. When the Philistine looked and saw David, he disdained him; for he was but a youth, and ruddy, with a handsome appearance. The Philistine said to David, "Am I a dog, that you come to me with sticks¿" And the Philistine cursed David by his gods. The Philistine also said to David, "Come to me, and I will give your flesh to the birds of the sky and the beasts of the field."

Then David said to the Philistine, "You come to me with a sword, a spear, and a javelin, but I come to you in the name of the LORD of hosts, the God of the armies of Israel, whom you have taunted. "This day the LORD will deliver you up into my hands, and I will strike you down and remove your head from you. And I will give the dead bodies of the army of the Philistines this day to the birds of the sky and the wild beasts of the earth, that all the earth may know that there is a God in Israel, and that all this assembly may know that the LORD does not deliver by sword or by spear; for the battle is the LORD'S and He will give you into our hands." Then it happened when the Philistine rose and came and drew near to meet David, that David ran quickly toward the battle line to meet the Philistine. And David put his hand into his bag and took from it a stone and slung it, and struck the Philistine on his forehead. And the stone sank into his forehead, so that he fell on his face to the ground. Thus David prevailed over the Philistine with a sling and a stone, and he struck the Philistine and killed him; but there was no sword in David's hand. Then David ran and stood over the Philistine and took his sword and drew it out of its sheath and killed him, and cut off his head with it. When the Philistines saw that their champion was dead, they fled. The men of Israel and Judah arose and shouted and pursued the Philistines as far as the valley, and to the gates of Ekron. And the slain Philistines lay along the way to Shaaraim, even to Gath and Ekron. The sons of Israel returned from chasing the Philistines and plundered their camps.

1 Samuel 17:40–53 (NASB)

David called his problem what it was, an uncircumcised Philistine, and he attacked it head on in the name of the Lord. He wasn't impressed by the size of his problem. He was in awe of the size of his God. He drew strength from his relationship with him. He remembered the way God had delivered him in the past and he trusted. He knew God was with him and for him. He trusted in God's character knowing he would not let him down.

HE <u>BELIEVED</u> GOD COULD DO MORE WITH A SMALL STONE IN A SURRENDERED HAND THAN A FORTIFIED GIANT COULD EVER DO.

Faith and character are proven through tests and trials. The problem named Goliath actually exposed where Israel needed to grow. They needed to grow in faith and their God given identity. The Israelites did not act in the faith that God was for them, would show up, or that he would fight the battle for them. On the other hand, David was fully confident that he was the Lord's anointed and when he stepped out against the enemy, God would show up. What made David different from everyone else?

TIME

He spent time with God. He had a personal and intimate relationship with God. His perspective on the problem named Goliath was God filtered.

At the beginning of *STRONGER* you identified areas where you needed strength. Problems in your life are opportunities for you to grow stronger in faith. They train you to trust that you can do all things through Christ who gives you strength (Philippians 4:13). They train you to believe that if God is for you nothing can stand against you (Romans 8:31). They show that his power and presence are available to you. They strengthen your faith. How we respond to problems is proof of what we believe.

- When problems invade your life, are you overcome with fear or faith?
- Do you avoid the issue allowing it to become bigger and stronger than it really is?
- Do you approach the battle expectantly?
- Do you bring the baggage of the past to the battle line?
- Do you trust in who God says you are or see yourself through man's eyes?
- Do you recognize the victories of the past and allow those to give you confidence?
- Do you know God's will and act accordingly?

Training to reign is part of your minute by minute walk with the Lord. He is constantly at work growing your faith and character. Each new day brings new opportunities to grow in faith as you become more like him. He is with you every step of your journey. He longs for you to grow in your understanding of his love for you. He wants you to trust and believe he is for you no matter what comes your way in life. He longs for you to be so rooted in him that you are not moved or shaken by the circumstances of life. He wants to give you more of his Spirit so you can walk confidently, aware of his will for you—his good, perfect and pleasing will for your life.

God's Heart for You

My Child,

I love you with an everlasting love. I lovingly lead you as a shepherd leads his flock. I lead you to rest in a lush tranquil place alongside calm waters. I will quiet your mind and give you my peace to restore and refresh your soul. I make your way easy so you are able to live according to my righteous ways. I do this for my own sake as your life brings me glory. Even when your path leads out of this earth you will not fear any evil because I am always with you. As your shepherd I will protect and comfort you every step of the way. Your enemies will see the abundant table I will set before you. I will anoint your head with oil and your cup will always remain full. My goodness and lovingkindness will fill all the days of your life and you will live safely in my house forever.

Dearest sons and daughters, consider it joyful when you face difficult times of any kind; I use these times to prove your faith. My goal is to strengthen your perseverance as you live in me. This perseverance will mature you and complete your growth in me. If you need wisdom, ask me; I will not find fault with your questions, I will answer you with an open heart full of love for you. I will be pleased to answer your questions. When you ask for wisdom, ask with faith and without doubts; anyone who doubts is like the ocean waves moved to and fro by the wind. People like this cannot expect to hear anything directly from me. Those without faith are not secure in me and are only keeping all their options open. Trust in me and I will give you the desires of your heart.

~~~~~~~~~~

Everlasting love; Jeremiah 31:3. As a shepherd leads his flock; John 10:1–18. Calm waters, peace, refresh your soul, abundant table, anoint head with oil, goodness, live in the Lord's house forever; Psalm 23. Bring me (God) glory; Exodus 34:10, Deuteronomy 28:1–14. Joy in difficulty proves faith, perseverance, maturity, ask for wisdom, do not doubt; James 1:2–8. Trust in me, I will give you the desires of your heart; Psalm 37:4.

SHARE

1. Review the lesson and discuss the questions that are interesting to your group.

2. If you haven't already, share your experience of your time spent with the Lord. What obstacles did you face and how are you overcoming them?

3. Share what you have learned from problems?

4. Our time together in this study is limited and soon we won't be reminding you weekly to stay on track. If you have established a strength training partner or two, consider keeping this relationship going. If you haven't established a training partner yet, seriously consider establishing this kind of relationship and check-in with each other at least twice a week for support. You only have one more week! Make it count!

STRENGTH TRAINING

GETTING STARTED:

This week we learned our faith is built in God as we defeat problems together with him. For your *Strength Training* exercise, practice the presence of God in the problems of life.

Read and meditate on Psalm 23.

> *The LORD is my shepherd; I have all that I need. He lets me rest in green meadows; he leads me beside peaceful streams. He renews my strength. He guides me along right paths, bringing honor to his name. Even when I walk through the darkest valley, I will not be afraid, for you are close beside me. Your rod and your staff protect and comfort me. You prepare a feast for me in the presence of my enemies. You honor me by anointing my head with oil. My cup overflows with blessings. Surely your goodness and unfailing love will pursue me all the days of my life, and I will live in the house of the LORD forever.*

Psalm 23:1–6 (NLT)

HEART CHECK:

> *For God has not given us a spirit of fear,*
> *but of power and of love and of a sound mind.*
> 2 Timothy 1:7 (NKJV)

If you are battling a problem and are experiencing fear ask the following questions. Answer thoughtfully. Ask the Lord to show you any misconceptions that could lead to *heart dis-ease* in his presence.

Begin with a HEART CHECK

- When problems invade your life are you overcome with fear or faith?
- Do you avoid the issue allowing it become bigger and stronger than it really is?
- Do you approach the battle expectantly?
- Do you bring the baggage of the past to the battle line?
- Do you trust in who God says you are or see yourself through man's eyes?
- Do you recognize the victories of the past and allow those to give you confidence?
- Do you know God's will and act accordingly?

HIS PRESENCE GIVES US PERSPECTIVE! PRACTICE IT!

DAILY EXERCISE: PRACTICING REST

Do what refreshes you daily while practicing his presence.

STEP ONE – DO WHAT YOU ENJOY!

- Remember to incorporate REST while doing what you enjoy.

  R = Relax

  E = Enter in

  S = Steep

  T = Talk with

- Spend time reflecting on what you have believed to be true about who God is, who you are in his sight, and how he relates to you.

This Works For Me!

What has really helped me to REST is to name my problem and call it out. Just like David, instead of being intimidated by the size and appearance of my Goliath, I call it what it is—an uncircumcised Philistine! I feel immediately empowered and capable. I remember Jesus has a plan for victory. The battle is already won. I must partner with him and act. —Diana

---

STEP TWO – BE AWARE!

Note what you are feeling or sensing.

- Are you comfortable? Are you restless? If so, ask why.
- Write down what comes to your mind.

Remember the goal is to be set free from anything that hinders deeper intimacy with God.

- Make sure you record what you learned, felt, or heard in your *Strength Training Journal*. Do you feel rested? Or are you feeling dis-ease?
Finally, talk with God about what you are learning.

MY STRENGTH TRAINING JOURNAL

Keep track of what you learned this week. Take notes so you can share PRACTICAL *Strength Training* tips with your group.

What I learned about myself this week:

What I learned about God this week:

What I learned about *Strength Training* this week:

LEVEL 6: JUST GAZE!

FOCUS

We're nearing the end of our journey together. Over the last five weeks you've learned how to become *stronger* in your relationship with the Lord. You've learned:

- The source of our all our strength (physical, emotional, and spiritual) is the Lord.

- Feeling busy, weary, and weak is a result of motion sickness.

- Rest is the antidote to motion sickness.

- Restlessness is a sign of *heart dis-ease* which is a condition rooted in fear caused by a misconception about who God is, how God sees you, and how he relates to you.

- Training to Reign and Giant Slaying are part of our Strength Training program.

- Character and faith are tested through your problems.

Most of all, you've learned to practice the presence of God. Only his presence provides us with the strength we need for each new day. In fact, the amount of our strength is dependent upon our awareness of his presence.

EXPLORE

Each person of the trinity provides you with strength.

FATHER

Don't be afraid, for I am with you. Don't be discouraged, for I am your God. I will strengthen you and help you. I will hold you up with my victorious right hand.
Isaiah 41:10 (NLT)

SON

But the Lord stood with me and gave me strength...
2 Timothy 4:17 (NLT)

HOLY SPIRIT

May He grant you out of the rich treasury of His glory to be strengthened and reinforced with mighty power in the inner man by the [Holy] Spirit [Himself indwelling your innermost being and personality].
Ephesians 3:16 (AMP)

THERE IS ONE FINAL RELATIONSHIP FROM WHICH WE DRAW STRENGTH.

But I have prayed especially for you [Peter], that your [own] faith may not fail; and when you yourself have turned again, strengthen and establish your brethren.
Luke 22:32 (AMP)

As disciples of Jesus we draw strength from the Spirit of God at work in other people. In relationship, we are able to draw strength from one another's faith journey. To strengthen our brethren, as Jesus encouraged Peter to do, we have to share our journey—our experiences, victories, and challenges. One of the core values of *STRONGER* is the idea we never strength train alone. We are *stronger* together in community.

Therefore encourage (admonish, exhort) one another and edify
(strengthen and build up) one another, just as you are doing.

1 Thessalonians 5:11 (AMP)

Strength flows from a community of Jesus followers who practice loving one another by encouraging and edifying. If we want to continue to grow in intimacy with the Lord, and if we want to continue to grow in the awareness of his presence and strength, then we must practice the *one anothers*. "One another" is mentioned over one hundred times in ninety four verses in the New Testament. Forty-seven of those are instructions given to followers of Jesus. The *one anothers* stress the importance of community in our walk with God. Each person who follows Jesus has a personal and unique walk with him. Because we are individuals, the way we strength train and practice the presence of God will look different. God is at work in my life and growing me, but it looks different than how he is at work in your life.

The beauty of individuality is that we can learn from, be encouraged, and even inspired by one another's individual journey. No two people grow at the same pace. No two people have exactly the same experiences. But…when you share your journey with me, I can learn something new about God, how he sees me, or how he relates to me through your experience. This is, in effect, *iron sharpening iron* (Proverbs 27:17). Our story is really God's story and it is used to:

- Comfort others

All praise to God, the Father of our Lord Jesus Christ. God is our merciful Father
and the source of all comfort. He comforts us in all our troubles so that we can comfort
others. When they are troubled, we will be able to give them the same comfort God
has given us. For the more we suffer for Christ, the more God will shower us with his
comfort through Christ. Even when we are weighed down with troubles, it is for your
comfort and salvation! For when we ourselves are comforted, we will certainly comfort
you. Then you can patiently endure the same things we suffer.

2 Corinthians 1:3–6 (NLT)

- Overcome the accuser of the brethren

> *Then I heard a loud voice in heaven say: "Now have come the salvation*
> *and the power and the kingdom of our God, and the authority of his Christ.*
> *For the accuser of our brothers, who accuses them before our God day and*
> *night, has been hurled down. They overcame him by the blood of the*
> *Lamb and by the word of their testimony...*
>
> Revelation 12:10–11 (NIV)

Our stories have power and this is why we are able to strengthen one another through our personal sharing.

DISCIPLINES ARE UNIVERSAL. EXPERIENCES ARE PERSONAL

Because we are different, the way we practice spiritual disciplines may be different. Spiritual disciplines include prayer, worship, Bible reading, fasting, practicing his presence, etc. We may find that one discipline strengthens us more than another. However, all work together to create intimacy with the Lord. We strengthen each other by sharing how God has strengthened us. While we each may have a different perspective about which discipline is most important to us, our desire for intimacy with him is the same.

To illustrate this point we interviewed four people about their experience with God as he led each one to practice a spiritual discipline that strengthened them. This is what we learned from each of them.

1. To grow stronger Pam said: STRENGTHEN YOURSELF IN HIS WORD
   - Hide the Word in your heart

> *Your word have I laid up in my heart, that I might not sin against You.*
>
> Psalm 119:11 (AMP)

   - Trust him to bring it to your remembrance

> *But the Comforter (Counselor, Helper, Intercessor, Advocate, Strengthener,*
> *Standby), the Holy Spirit, Whom the Father will send in My name [in*
> *My place, to represent Me and act on My behalf], He will teach you*

all things. And He will cause you to recall (will remind you of,
bring to your remembrance) everything I have told you.

John 14:26 (AMP)

CJ asked Pam, "How has the Word strengthened you?"

"I have grown through Bible study, reading the Word, and practicing inductive study skills. I have learned to talk with God as I study; I ask what each verse means and how to apply it to my life. I have listened intently to him, seeking and searching for understanding. This has helped me to follow him. I've grown the most through my personal time with him in his Word. Years and years of Bible study has filled my heart and my mind with his truth. I am intimately familiar with it, and it has gone down deep into my spirit. I feel encouraged and stronger as I listen to him. My ability to endure has come from my commitment to search his Word and apply his Truth."

CJ asked Pam, "How might someone strengthen themselves in the Word?"

"Read the Bible with a pen or pencil in hand. Highlight or mark what stands out. Practice active reading—think of Bible reading as a conversation you're having with God."

2. To grow stronger Karrie said: STRENGTHEN YOURSELF THROUGH OBEDIENCE
    *   Obedience is the evidence of love for God

        This is love for God: to obey his commands.
        And his commands are not burdensome...

        1 John 5:3 (NIV)

    *   Obedience is not difficult if you are led by the Spirit

        And I will put my Spirit in you so that you will follow my
        decrees and be careful to obey my regulations.

        Ezekiel 36:27 (NLT)

CJ asked Karrie, "How has obedience strengthened you?"

"Obedience opens the door for me to experience more of him. When God has told me what to do I have learned to obey. I am actually more afraid to disobey God. I know a blessing is coming, a reward, when I am obedient to him. As I spend time in his presence, I have the strength to obey. When I spend time with him, my spirit is infused with his Spirit and I am able to overcome my flesh, which always wants what is opposite of what God wants for me. Spending time with him is the key to obedience. I have to allow his Spirit to lead me, which means I have to choose. When he said "rest," I rested, and there were spiritual blessings that came from rest, such as, peace, stronger relationships, better health, etc."

CJ asked Karrie, "How might someone strengthen themselves through obedience?"

"Encourage yourself in the Lord! The Word is life, so encourage yourself by reading the Word. Bury the Word in your heart so you know what the Bible says. That way you will recognize God's voice as the Spirit speaks to you. The Holy Spirit will bring his Word to you when you need it most and it strengthens you and guides you. This is not your memory, this is the Holy Spirit at work in you."

3: To grow stronger Francesca said: PRACTICE LOVE

- Love is the evidence we belong to him

> *By this all men will know that you are my*
> *disciples, if you love one another.*
>
> John 13:35 (NIV)

- Love is the most important virtue

> *If I could speak all the languages of earth and of angels, but didn't*
> *love others, I would only be a noisy gong or a clanging cymbal.*
> *If I had the gift of prophecy, and if I understood all of God's secret*
> *plans and possessed all knowledge, and if I had such faith that*
> *I could move mountains, but didn't love others, I would be nothing.*
> *If I gave everything I have to the poor and even sacrificed*
> *my body, I could boast about it; but if I didn't love others,*

I would have gained nothing. Love is patient and kind. Love is not jealous or boastful or proud or rude. It does not demand its own way. It is not irritable, and it keeps no record of being wronged. It does not rejoice about injustice but rejoices whenever the truth wins out. Love never gives up, never loses faith, is always hopeful, and endures through every circumstance."

1 Corinthians 13:1–7 (NLT)

- Love covers

Above all things have intense and unfailing love for one another, for love covers a multitude of sins [forgives and disregards the offenses of others].

1 Peter 4:8 (AMP)

CJ asked Francesca, "How has practicing love strengthened you?"

"Keeping short accounts has opened my mind and heart to growing stronger by loving others. So often what I thought was said wasn't really what someone meant. God has taught me to trust him which has given me the ability to be more honest in my relationships. I have learned, instead of drawing my own conclusions about what people said or meant, I can allow myself to be vulnerable and approach others for clarity and understanding. I can do this in confidence knowing I am secure in him. Because he has strengthened me with his love, I have the ability to love others more freely, without all the baggage of the past. I can now say to someone, "I sense that you're upset with me, is that true? I can now say to someone, "I was wondering when you said _____ did I offend you? I can even just blurt out "Oh, did I just shame you? I'm sorry." I'm able to tackle one of my giants, relational issues, because God has strengthened me with his love. His love equips me to love others. His love has strengthened my relationships."

CJ asked Francesca, "How might someone practice loving others?"

"Start practicing with someone you know and trust. Love by asking clarifying questions when communication is hurtful or unclear. Give others the benefit of the doubt. And most of all keep short accounts. In other words, don't let too much time pass before you talk to someone. Trust the Lord to give you the words and his love when dealing with people."

4. To grow stronger Julie said: STRENGTHEN YOURSELF THROUGH PRAYER
   - Ask - Pray the word from a posture of absolute assurance

     Ask and it will be given to you; seek and you will find; knock
     and the door will be opened to you. For everyone who asks
     receives; he who seeks finds; and to him who knocks, the door
     will be opened. Which of you, if his son asks for bread,
     will give him a stone? Or if he asks for a fish, will give
     him a snake? If you, then, though you are evil, know how
     to give good gifts to your children, how much more will your
     Father in heaven give good gifts to those who ask him!

     Matthew 7:7–11 (NIV)

   - Believe

     Now faith is being sure of what we hope for
     and certain of what we do not see.

     Hebrews 11:1 (NIV)

   - Receive

     And Jesus answered saying to them, "Have faith in God. Truly
     I say to you, whoever says to this mountain, 'Be taken up and
     cast into the sea,' and does not doubt in his heart, but believes
     that what he says is going to happen, it will be granted him.
     Therefore I say to you, all things for which you pray
     and ask, believe that you have received them,
     and they will be granted you."

     Mark 11:22–24 (NASB)

- Praise

> *Be anxious for nothing, but in everything by prayer and*
> *supplication with thanksgiving let your requests be made*
> *known to God. And the peace of God, which surpasses*
> *all comprehension, will guard your hearts and*
> *your minds in Christ Jesus.*
>
> Philippians 4:6–7 (NASB)

CJ asked Julie, "How has prayer strengthened you?"

"Prayer brought me out of an emotional state into a stable state based on the Word of God. I would pray, calling out to God asking him to help me and be there for me. Then I would stop and just end my prayer. I finally realized I was only expressing emotion. It is okay for me to state my need but then I need to pray the Word over my situation and stand in faith. I needed to believe his promises over my emotion. As a result I've grown stronger in my faith. Because my prayer is rooted in the Word of God I have assurance when I pray. It is a process, but I know God is my rock."

CJ asked Julie, "How might some practice praying in faith?"

"Practice the steps I learned in my process that brought me to a place of victory in my life. I ask, believe, receive and praise!"

5. To grow stronger I, CJ, say: STRENGTHEN YOURSELF BY SEEKING GOD FIRST

- Seek his Kingdom Come

> *But seek first His kingdom and His righteousness,*
> *and all these things will be added to you.*
>
> Matthew 6:33 (NASB)

- Watch your priorities

> *Whom have I in heaven but You? And besides You,*
> *I desire nothing on earth. My flesh and my heart may fail,*
> *But God is the strength of my heart and my portion forever.*

Psalm 73:25–26 (NASB)

How has seeking God first strengthened me?

"I am not ashamed to tell you that there have been times in my life when my priorities have been out of line. Slowly God slipped from first place in my heart while the concerns of life took front and center. However, God is so good to remind me through his Word, the Spirit within, and the community of Jesus followers in my life, that my desire needs to be only for him. When I seek him first, when he is my one and only desire, my heart is strengthened. He is everything, everything I need. As I experience contentment in his presence balance returns to my life. Anxiety, fear, stress, and the temptation to control subside and his peace and love overwhelm me."

How might someone grow stronger through keeping God first?

"Start with self-examination. What matters most to you? Does God come before or after what matters most? How do you feel; are you peaceful or stressed? Practice balance by keeping God first in your heart. Seek his presence. Rest in him. Don't forget to Just Gaze upon the beauty of Lord. Seek his presence as your most vital need (Psalm 27).

And on those days when you struggle to connect with the Lord, when you feel weak, allow the words of Psalm 139 to encourage you."

> *O LORD, you have examined my heart and know everything about me. You know*
> *when I sit down or stand up. You know my thoughts even when I'm far away. You*
> *see me when I travel and when I rest at home. You know everything I do. You*
> *know what I am going to say even before I say it, LORD. You go before me*
> *and follow me. You place your hand of blessing on my head. Such*
> *knowledge is too wonderful for me, too great for me to understand!*

Psalm 139:1–6 (NLT)

STOP – Write down what you are feeling, sensing, hearing, or seeing.

I can never escape from your Spirit! I can never get away from your presence!
If I go up to heaven, you are there; if I go down to the grave, you are there.
If I ride the wings of the morning, if I dwell by the farthest oceans, even
there your hand will guide me, and your strength will support me.
I could ask the darkness to hide me and the light around me to become
night—but even in darkness I cannot hide from you. To you the night
shines as bright as day. Darkness and light are the same to you.

Psalm 139:7–12 (NLT)

STOP – Write down what you are feeling, sensing, hearing, or seeing.

For you created my inmost being; you knit me together in my mother's womb.
I praise you because I am fearfully and wonderfully made; your works are
wonderful, I know that full well. My frame was not hidden from you
when I was made in the secret place. When I was woven together in the
depths of the earth, your eyes saw my unformed body. All the days ordained
for me were written in your book before one of them came to be.

Psalm 139:13–16 (NIV)

STOP – Write down what you are feeling, sensing, hearing, or seeing.

How precious are your thoughts about me, O God. They cannot be numbered!
I can't even count them; they outnumber the grains of sand!
And when I wake up, you are still with me!

Psalm 139:17–18 (NLT)

STOP – Write down what you are feeling, sensing, hearing, or seeing.

O God, if only you would destroy the wicked! Get out of my life, you murderers!
They blaspheme you; your enemies misuse your name. O LORD, shouldn't I hate
those who hate you? Shouldn't I despise those who oppose you? Yes, I hate them
with total hatred, for your enemies are my enemies. Search me, O God, and know
my heart; test me and know my anxious thoughts. Point out anything in me that
offends you, and lead me along the path of everlasting life.

Psalm 139:19–24 (NLT)

STOP – Write down what you are feeling, sensing, hearing, or seeing.

If you will incorporate the above practices into your life on a regular basis you will learn to recognize the voice of the Lord. Friends, he speaks to you. He loves you. He longs for you to come to him and experience the joy of REST in his presence. You can cultivate intimacy with God. You can strengthen your faith. You can defeat *heart dis-ease.* You can eliminate doubts and the fears that tempt you to run from God. You can trust him completely.

He is waiting for you.

*I pray that from his glorious, unlimited resources he will empower you with inner
strength through his Spirit. Then Christ will make his home in your hearts as you
trust in him. Your roots will grow down into God's love and keep you strong. And
may you have the power to understand, as all God's people should, how wide,
how long, how high, and how deep his love is. May you experience the love of Christ,
though it is too great to understand fully. Then you will be made complete with all
the fullness of life and power that comes from God. Now all glory to God, who
is able, through his mighty power at work within us, to accomplish infinitely
more than we might ask or think. Glory to him in the church and in
Christ Jesus through all generations forever and ever! Amen.*

Ephesians 3:16–21 (NLT)

GODS HEART FOR YOU

My child, keep your eyes on me. Don't let anything rock your focus off of me; I will never leave or forsake you. Do not fear times of trial or hardship, for I am always with you and I will strengthen and help you. I always stand with you; I strengthen you by my Holy Spirit dwelling deep within you. When you realize your strength comes from me, you will be able to strengthen and establish many brothers and sisters in Christ for my glory. Therefore, embrace every circumstance and experience as an opportunity to learn and receive from me. Then, as I have comforted you, continue to comfort and encourage one another just as you have been comforted. Do not be timid about sharing your journey in me with others. Your experiences, both joys and suffering, have the power to encourage and strengthen many who cross your path. Do not despise the times when you do not understand my ways. My ways are not your ways. I do not allow anything to touch your life that does not draw you to me for strength; my will is always to strengthen you in me.

My Word is your greatest source of strength; by knowing and embracing its truths you become more like me. As you take in my Word I am able to bring it to your remembrance when your experiences require my wisdom and strength. As you grow in your ability to obey my Word you also grow in your ability to love, your love for me is revealed by the way you are able to love others. My Spirit leads you into greater obedience as you grow in your ability to experience more of me.

Prayer is the doorway for intimate communication and relationship with me. Make time to hear my voice. I long to show you wonderful things, things beyond your own imagination. Ask of me and I will not disappoint you, believe in faith that I hear and answer you. All things for which you pray and ask, believe that you have received them, and my peace, which surpasses all comprehension, will guard your heart and your mind in Christ Jesus.

Make no other gods before me, desire nothing more than you desire true intimacy with me and I will give you my kingdom and righteousness. There is nothing on earth worthy of your desire; I alone can satisfy the deepest longings of your heart.

Now come closer to me. Seek more of my presence. Come to me and let's do life together. Allow me to strengthen you and fill you with the fullness of joy.

> *Seek the LORD and His strength; Seek His face continually.*
> 1 Chronicles 16:11 (NASB)

> *I love you, LORD; you are my strength.*
> Psalm 18:1 (NLT)

~~~~~~~~~~

I will never leave you; Deuteronomy 31:6, Matthew 28:20. Times of hardship, discipline; Hebrews 12:1–12. Peace of mind and comfort; Matthew 11:29, Philippians 4:9. Comfort; 2 Corinthians 1:3–5, Philippians 2:1–4. Our thoughts are not God's thoughts; Isaiah 55:7–9. Holy Spirit, comfort, obey Jesus' teaching; John 14:15–27. God's Word; Psalm 119:104–106. Prayer, Ask, God will show you; Luke 11:1–13, Mark 11:24–26, Philippians 4:4–9, Jeremiah 33:3. No other gods before me; Exodus 20:3ff. Come to me; Matthew 11:27–30.

SMALL GROUP EXERCISE

1. Overall, what is your biggest take-away from your time in this *STRONGER* study?

2. How has your perspective of quiet time and *true intimacy with God* changed over the course of the past six weeks? What, if anything, will be different for you going forward?

3. From the *personal experiences* you read, what thoughts or encouragements helped you and why?

4. As you think back over what it means to be *stronger*, how have you grown the most because of the perspective you now have about being *stronger*?

5. If you can't really say that you have a better understanding about how true spiritual strength is available to you; what do you think is your biggest obstacle? How can you overcome this obstacle?

APPENDIX

CJ Rapp Bio

In 2003, CJ Rapp began inspiring and strengthening women on their journey to find healing and hope. Her mission is to establish women in their identity as God's beloved and help them experience greater intimacy with Jesus.

As a masterpiece in progress, CJ learned to embrace what she calls the beautiful work of brokenness in life. She is familiar with the heartache of rejection, the sting of unkind words and the nagging need to control. She knows the struggle to measure up, the difficulty of getting along with others, and the challenge to "keep the faith" in the midst of life's storms. In short, she "gets it." CJ says her friendship with Jesus, the love of her Daddy God, and the power of Holy Spirit is the sustaining force of her life. She sees every circumstance as an opportunity to trust and believe in the goodness of God.

As a gifted communicator, CJ will touch your heart with her authentic, casual style, make you laugh, renew your hope and inspire you with her passion for and insight into God's Word. An expert in women's issues, she specializes in ruin prevention and repair. Her heart is to help women revolutionize their life by re-defining their self-image and refining their understanding of God's heart for them. CJ is the author several books, including the heart touching women's devotional, *I AM Says, "You Are..." Understanding Your Identity in Christ.* She has also written articles for the Christian Post as well as other magazines. She frequently speaks at retreats, conferences, and workshops around the country.

CJ's experience includes serving as a ministry leader in a mega-church in Southern California where she led over three hundred women in a weekly study. In 2012, feeling called to help women all over the world, she launched a national conference series entitled Trash the Lies. Today, she serves as a core team leader and teacher for Carport Community Church, an outreach ministry in Santa Ana, California. She is the founder and Chief Executive Officer of CJ Rapp Ministries, Inc., a 501C3 whose mission is based on the promises found in Isaiah 61 to "bind up the brokenhearted and proclaim freedom for the captives." CJ is also the President of Cherished Inc. which connects people with the resources and relationships that lead to transformation. In addition to offering workshops, conferences, and spiritual coaching, Cherished helps people connect with social service resources, drug and alcohol rehabs, and essential living necessities. She regularly donates her books to battered women's shelters, addiction recovery centers, and prisons across the country.

CJ is an advocate of soul care for leaders. She serves women in ministry by providing coaching, support and training.

CJ married her best friend John in 1998. Together they have two teenage boys, which provide a continuous source of character lessons and joy. As a family, they seek to live out their faith in an ever changing culture.

PAM MAROTTA BIO

Pam is a gifted communicator of God's written Word.

Her passion is to equip women to study the Word of God for themselves. If asked, she will tell you her ministry is HUGS.

She longs for women to experience the love Jesus has for them. Pam's experience includes writing Bible studies for Saddleback Church and Life Together. For the last decade she has served alongside CJ as the Project Manager and Executive Producer for Infusion Publishing.

She is the co-author of *Tossed, Tumbled and Still Trusting, Trash the Lies*, and *Stronger—A Simple Guide for Connecting with God.*

LIST OF STRONGER EXERCISES

Tossed, Tumbled and Still Trusting
A study in the Book of Ruth

by CJ Rapp and Pam Marotta

Can you image how you would react if you lost everything; your spouse, home, comfort, security, and children?

These are the very situations God allowed into the lives of two prominent women of the Bible, Ruth and Naomi. Perhaps you have experienced a similar loss or trial and you too have questioned, "Why? God."

Tests and trials not only challenge our faith, they reveal our character—who we are when no one is watching.

Explore the actions and reactions of Ruth and Naomi to their most difficult life struggles. Learn to identify character imperfections and replace them with Christ-like attitudes and behavior. Come to know that despite being tossed and tumbled by life, you can choose to be like Ruth, a woman of excellence.

Learn to rise above your feelings, cling to your faith, and believe God for more than what you see.

Tossed, Tumbled and Still Trusting, features three days of heart-work per lesson, weekly group discussion sessions for any size small group or centralized group, and a leader guide with step-by-step instructions for facilitating nine group sessions.

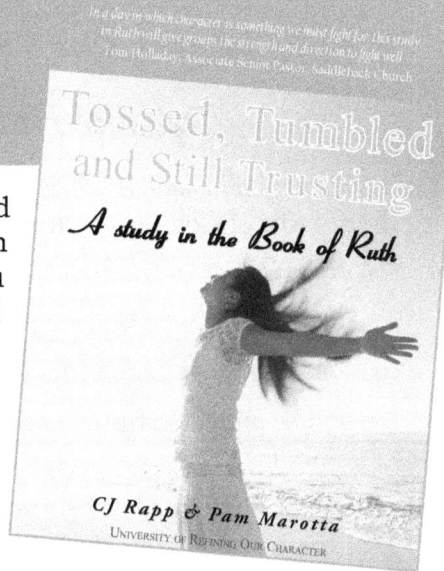

Infusion P·U·B·L·I·S·H·I·N·G
A Ministry of Unfading Beauty Ministries

Price:	$19.95
Binding:	Paperback
Pages:	184
Size:	8.5 x 11
ISBN-13:	978-0982479032

Coming Soon!

Treasure Hunters—Philippians

Treasure Hunters—Philippians will lead you on the most exciting adventure of your life—a journey to the heart of God. As you mine the Scriptures, you will discover vast riches:

- You will uncover truths about God's heart and character.

- You will find out who you are in Christ and just how God sees you.

- You will learn how God wants you to live as his treasured possession.

- You will be protected from false teaching because you will have uncovered the truth for yourself.

Treasure Hunters is designed to help you learn a method of study that equips you to mine the Word for the treasures it holds. Based on the inductive method of Bible study, *Treasure Hunters* focuses on building the study skills of observation, interpretation, and application into your study habits.

www.ingramcontent.com/pod-product-compliance
Lightning Source LLC
LaVergne TN
LVHW061224060426
835509LV00012B/1419